PITCH PERFECT

RAISING CAPITAL FOR YOUR STARTUP

Haje Jan Kamps

Apress®

Pitch Perfect

Haje Jan Kamps
Oakland, CA, USA

ISBN-13 (pbk): 978-1-4842-6064-7   ISBN-13 (electronic): 978-1-4842-6065-4
https://doi.org/10.1007/978-1-4842-6065-4

Managing Director, Apress Media LLC: Welmoed Spahr
Acquisitions Editor: Shiva Ramachandran
Development Editor: Matthew Moodie
Coordinating Editor: Nancy Chen

Cover designed by eStudioCalamar

Distributed to the book trade worldwide by Springer Science+Business Media New York, 1 New York Plaza, New York, NY 100043. Phone 1-800-SPRINGER, fax (201) 348-4505, e-mail orders-ny@springer-sbm.com, or visit www.springeronline.com. Apress Media, LLC is a California LLC and the sole member (owner) is Springer Science + Business Media Finance Inc (SSBM Finance Inc). SSBM Finance Inc is a **Delaware** corporation.

For information on translations, please e-mail booktranslations@springernature.com; for reprint, paperback, or audio rights, please e-mail bookpermissions@springernature.com.

Apress titles may be purchased in bulk for academic, corporate, or promotional use. eBook versions and licenses are also available for most titles. For more information, reference our Print and eBook Bulk Sales web page at http://www.apress.com/bulk-sales.

Any source code or other supplementary material referenced by the author in this book is available to readers on GitHub via the book's product page, located at www.apress.com/978-1-4842-6064-7. For more detailed information, please visit http://www.apress.com/source-code.

Printed on acid-free paper

For founders.
You say "yes" to a hell of a journey.

Contents

About the Author vii

Acknowledgments ix

Introduction xi

Chapter 1:   Storytelling 1

Chapter 2:   How Venture Capital Works 9

Chapter 3:   Pitch Deck Design 15

Chapter 4:   What Slides Will You Need? 21

Chapter 5:   Slide: The Problem 27

Chapter 6:   Slide: The Solution 31

Chapter 7:   Slide: The Product 35

Chapter 8:   Slide: Market 39

Chapter 9:   Slide: Team 43

Chapter 10:   Slide: Traction 47

Chapter 11:   Slide: The Moat 53

Chapter 12:   Slide: Business Model 57

Chapter 13:   Slide: Go-to-Market Strategy 61

Chapter 14:   Slide: Competitors 65

Chapter 15:   Slide: The Ask 69

Chapter 16:   Slide: Timing 75

Chapter 17:   The Take-Home Deck 79

Chapter 18:   Who Should You Be Talking To? 83

Chapter 19:   Getting Introductions 89

Chapter 20:   The Investment Thesis 93

Chapter 21:   Further Reading 97

Index 101

About the Author

Haje Jan Kamps is an experienced author, entrepreneur, speaker, and business advisor. He has written a stack of books about photography and life in Silicon Valley. His books have been translated into a dozen languages.

Frequently on the speaking circuit, Haje has been on stage in the United Kingdom, Norway, Denmark, Russia, Israel, Iceland, and the United States, talking about various aspects of entrepreneurship. Alongside his own books, he has also ghostwritten a number of books for influential entrepreneurs and investors in the San Francisco Bay Area.

Haje founded and/or helped build four companies, including a hardware company in the photography space (Triggertrap), a Software-as-a-Service marketing company (ScreenCloud), a chatbot company that helped people have their very first conversation about death (LifeFolder), and the very first photography news site in Norway (Digitalkamera.no). These days, he is working on a new venture called Konf, building the future of virtual events—see Konf.co.

Over the past decade, he has mentored more than a hundred startups, and he has seen thousands of pitches—the good, the bad, and the ugly. In addition to his entrepreneurial efforts, Haje is working as a founder coach (see haje.me), helping startup founders build companies that stand the test of time, and—yes—create perfect pitches.

Author photo by Auey Santos - AueySantos.com

Acknowledgments

A huge thanks to Ben, Vitaly, Kate, Greg, and Axel, who all helped me find my feet in the world of venture capital.

Introduction

You have it. The perfect idea for a company is crystallizing in your mind. Early research indicates that the journey you are embarking on could be both fun, challenging, lucrative, and engaging. Things are coming together beautifully. And now it's time to raise some money.

This book is focused on the pitch process; it is a guide to how to put together an extraordinary pitch. It will help you create an excellent narrative for your potential investors. But it is much more, too. It will help explain what parts of the story will be most potent in how you can raise money. It will discuss different ways of thinking about how to craft your story and how you can catch your target audience by surprise.

As with all great storytelling, you need to know your audience. You have to understand how investors think and what the driving forces are behind making an investment. To successfully raise money from institutional investors, you need to understand how venture capital (VC) works (Chapter 2). You need to know how to structure your fundraising story (Chapter 1). And you need to have the documents that back up your pitch and fundraising deck (Chapter 20).

Fundraising is a complicated process with many moving parts. Buried deep in the intersection of the people you've attracted to help build your business, the market you're going to be operating in, and the problem you are solving, there's a story. You are going to move the world from where you are today to the universe you can imagine in the future. To do that, you're going to deploy some resources, including money.

A startup fundraising pitch is designed to do one thing exceptionally effectively: paint a comprehensive picture of your company and the economy it operates in. Your potential investors will look at your pitch deck and listen to your pitch. A compelling story will make investors lean in and hitch their wagon to your dreams. An excellent presentation anticipates everything an investor will want to know about your venture. Both the great—the things you are better at than anybody else—and the not-so-great. In this book, I will dissect all the slides that typically appear in support of a pitch deck. I will talk about the things that throw up red flags for investors and about the things that are positive indicators for fundraising. I will take you behind the scenes of the decision-making process investors use to help you craft the best story possible.

The truth is that pitching is brutal: Laying your whole business bare in under 20 minutes means that there's no space for "fluff," and there will be very little to hide behind. Investors see dozens of pitches per week and are extraordinarily attuned to how this format works. If you are padding or beating about the bush, if you're lucky, they will call you on it. If you are less fortunate, the investors will tune out and mentally write you off long before you make it to the end of your story.

When I do pitch coaching, the "nowhere to hide" aspect becomes apparent all the time. Sometimes, when a founder stumbles over a slide or a part of the story, there's a simple fix. Perhaps a point needs to be set up earlier in the presentation. Maybe the story is cleaner if you don't delve as deep into a particular aspect of the business.

Surprisingly often, though, working with founders on their pitch decks doesn't show the shortcomings of the presentations. Instead, it reveals cracks in the foundation of the company itself—flaws in the go-to-market strategy and/or weaknesses in the team. Market dynamics that don't pan out or obvious flaws in the pricing or business model that prevent the business from being viable. A book can't cover every eventuality in where your company goes wrong— that's where my coaching practice comes in—but I will teach you the thought processes to help you self-assess.

A Guide to How to Help Yourself

You can't trust investors to tell you where your story falls apart. They are incredibly busy people. Some investors are willing to give you a nudge in the right direction, but in my experience, they don't have the bandwidth to engage in a long back-and-forth to fully ascertain the challenges in your pitch. They are in the business of investing and helping grow the 0.5% of companies they end up investing in, not fixing the underlying architectural challenges in the 99.5% they choose not to invest in.

Many investors are much more likely to give you a "soft no," which usually comes in the form of a "you're too early for us to invest," or "we don't focus on this market right now," or "please check back with us when you have some more traction." The complicated thing about the "soft no" is that it may be genuine: the investment firm may really want you to check back when you have a bit more traction, or they may actually be defocusing from the market you are talking about. However, investors are in the business of finding extraordinary humans building spectacular companies. In my experience, they will engage in conversations with companies, even if they aren't a slam dunk, if the opportunity is good enough. FOMO (fear of missing out) runs deep in the venture world, and a lot of the time, however, the "soft no" serves another purpose. It exists to help the firm have an option to talk to you again further down the line. If you find yourself getting a lot of soft nos, it probably means that there's something about the business that's not fully working.

I will help you find your voice and the story that will help your company come together in the eyes of an investor. In the process, I will give you the tools to look at your own company with the objectivity and criticism it needs. If there's a hole in the story, there's no point in going on the fundraising trail. You'll never raise money, and—more important, still—you'll waste months of your time.

We will also cover how to choose investors (Chapter 19), how to approach investors, how to source warm introductions, and how to make an unforgettable first impression.

This book is for anyone hoping to raise early-stage money from angel investors or venture capital investors—typically in the range of $150k–$10m. If you've pitched companies many times before, you'll learn a ton of additional tools for how to make your story come to life. If this is your first time through the mill, you're in good hands too. This is a comprehensive guide to the what, when, why, and how of how to raise money.

You're ready to take on the world. And it all starts with the perfect pitch.

Storytelling

... And why a great story is so important

You may be tempted to believe that investors invest with their brains. They gather all the information available about a company, the market, and the surrounding big picture, plug it all into a spreadsheet, and then decide whether to invest or not. That isn't the case, for two closely related reasons. The first reason is that investors are human, and humans naturally love stories and narratives. Being able to paint a picture of the problem you've perceived, how you're going to address that problem, and how the world is going to be different once the problem is solved is tapping into an emotional realm. Don't get me wrong; your investors will still do their "due diligence" and plug all the numbers you give them into spreadsheets to see if the story works on that level. But you can't skip the storytelling step: just handing someone a worksheet with all the numbers already filled in would only work for a vanishingly small subset of investors.

The other reason is that you, the entrepreneur, are human. The investors are not investing in a business plan or even a pitch—they are investing in you, personally. As you go through the fundraising process, you'll sit eye to eye with several extraordinarily smart people. They will try to figure out what makes you tick. Do you have what it takes to conjure this project from thin air? Are you able to attract and lead people who can help you along the way? Entrepreneurship is exceedingly hard—do you have what it takes to keep on the right track as everything in the world conspires against your company's success? And, ultimately, these investors are going to be literally and figuratively

© Haje Jan Kamps 2020
H. J. Kamps, *Pitch Perfect*, https://doi.org/10.1007/978-1-4842-6065-4_1

invested in your startup. They'll be on your board of directors, offering you direction and advice. One of the things they'll be looking for is whether you are coachable.

They will want you to have answers to many questions, but more importantly, they'll want to know how you arrive at those answers. How do you react when they ask you a question you don't have the answer to? Do you lie? Do you make up an answer on the spot? Do you get defensive? Do you say you don't know and promise to get back to them ASAP with a solution? You'll be unsurprised to learn that only one of those is the right thing to do. And you may be appalled to learn how many founders will make up an answer on the spot to seem knowledgeable—unaware that they're burning their credibility to the ground in the process.

As humans, we relate to each other in many different ways. In the world of fundraising, storytelling and conversations are the tools of the trade.

So, what IS storytelling?

There are as many blueprints for storytelling as there are stories. One of my favorite examples is "Married Life"—the montage that covers the first 10 minutes of the Pixar movie *Up*. In those 10 minutes, the filmmakers tell the story of the married life between Carl and Ellie. It consists of a series of brief vignettes from a lifelong marriage, ending in Ellie's death. If you've never seen it, you simply must. Without any of the characters saying a word, it tells a story of connection and love. It frequently leaves the whole audience in tears. The lesson you can learn from Married Life is that if you're able to tap into someone's dreams, fears, and sense of beauty, you can have a powerful connection with them.

The goal of your pitch isn't to have to hand out Kleenex at the end of your pitch because everyone is sobbing their eyes out, but it wouldn't be a wrong goal to at least try to evoke an emotion. Why is this problem so personally important to you? Why is there a significant shift in the world if you can implement these solutions? Who is the customer, and how does your company's existence impact their life?

Explicitly encouraging the investors to buy into your dream is one thing. Weaving a narrative that means that they can't help but dream along with you is a different league of engagement. I've sat in pitches where the whole room is enthralled, leaning in, eager to learn more. A magnetic, charismatic personality goes a long way—but even if you lack that, a great story that helps people envision the world the way you do is powerful.

Meet BeerSub.com

Figure 1-1. The opening slide for the company we'll be pitching throughout our book—BeerSub.com. Image Source: Alexander Raths/stock.adobe.com

In this book, I'm going to create the pitch for a company and take you along for the journey (see Figure 1-1). The company is BeerSub.com—a fictional beer delivery service raising a seed round.

I chose this fictional company for a couple of reasons. It is a business-to-consumer (B2C) company that is relatively easy to understand. I'm a fan of craft beer, so that helps, but more importantly, the direct-to-consumer (DTC) industry has seen a rapid rise over the past decade. Brands like Dollar Shave Club (razors), Casper (mattresses), and Blue Apron (dinner kits) have seen stratospheric rises.

Obviously, I haven't started this company in the real world, so I've had to get creative in some places. Of course, traction is particularly easy with a made-up company, but where possible, I have tried to keep figures plausible, at least. The important part of BeerSub—and its accompanying slides—isn't the specifics, but the broad strokes of how I'm telling the company's story.

The words and the pictures

Later in this book, we will explore how your slide deck can be used to back up the story you're telling. I wanted to say something about the interplay between your slide deck and your description before I get that far, however.

In an ideal world, your audience is on you—not on your slide deck. Of course, slides can do things you can't do with words: show photos of your product, show graphs of your process, and help punctuate the story you are telling.

A great slide deck is an essential tool for you to structure and underline the critical parts of your presentation. And a great storyteller doesn't need a slide deck. With one of my companies—Life Folder—we were creating a chatbot that was helping people have their very first conversation about death. In the pitch process, I would sit down, put my laptop on the table, and ask a question: "I have a slide deck, but we are about to talk about death for an hour. Do you want the deck, or shall we just chat?" Without fail, every investor had already received the deck in advance. Most of them had looked at it for long enough to decide to take the meeting, at least. And none—not a single one—out of the dozens of meetings I took wanted to see the deck. They wanted to look me in the eyes and engage at a different level. There's no way I would have been able to give an excellent presentation without using the deck as a mental crutch—but by the time these meetings were happening, I knew the performance off by heart; I had all the stats, talking points, and story points at my disposal. And, as I had expected, the investors found it far better to engage at a human-to-human level when talking about a difficult topic.

How to weave a story

If you've ever seen a truly great stand-up comedian, you'll have seen how they tell many small stories that are part of a much bigger whole. They get laughs in the short term, but the funniest jokes tend to be the ones that they've set up several minutes in advance. In the storytelling world, those techniques are called "gates" and "callbacks." The gates are story elements you have to pass through for the story to make sense later on—if you didn't set up the joke, the punch line doesn't make sense. The callbacks are more advanced jokes. Here, you tie up a loose thread that you dropped a while back—your quick-witted audience members see the gag coming, and the tension builds. When you finally get to the punch line, the audience experiences a sense of release and relief.

Your venture capital pitch should be like this, as well. For each slide, there will be one or two key points that you have to make. If you don't, the rest of the story falls apart. It is building upon itself throughout, so if you failed to mention something in an earlier part of the story, the rest of the narrative doesn't work. That is annoying if you catch yourself and can go back a couple of steps—but remember that you will be giving this pitch many, many times. Make sure you are well rehearsed. Failure to practice means that you might end up forgetting to mention key parts of your story. If that happens, at best, you will be facing needless questions. At worst, you'll meet the blank stare of someone who doesn't "get" your pitch.

The way to solve this is to think about the narrative and of the "gates" you need to hit. Mentally, keep track of what the next gate is, and gently guide your story in that direction. It sounds confusing, but it becomes a lot easier with practice. When you're presenting from slides, you can use them as a prompt to yourself, but the goal is to have a mental checklist ready.

For example, for one of my companies, I had "my background, their background, origin story, and hiring pipeline" as mental notes for my "team" slide. Earlier in the presentation, on the product page, I mention that we had a unique advantage of team recruitment—that both my co-founder and I had teams that we could bring with us. Explaining the specifics of that wasn't part of that slide—but it is a crucial part of the team slide. I know there are four talking points to hit when it comes to my team. A longer way of thinking of those talking points would be: "When I am talking about the team, I should mention my background and that that of my co-founders, highlighting how we have different but extremely well-matched skill sets. I should mention how long I've known my co-founders and how we have faced huge obstacles together in the past. If the mood in the room is right, tell the story of how we met. Remind the investor that we have 15 people kept warm who are ready to join the company, so hiring is a less-than-usual risk for this startup."

Everyone thinks about narrative a little bit differently, so how you make and organize your mental notes may be a bit different from how I would do it, but when you are practicing your pitch, it can't harm to use some index cards. Write the name of the slide at the top, and add some bullet points that remind you of the points you want to make here. Having a visual reminder of how many gates you have for each chapter of the narrative you're sharing is helpful when practicing.

Keep your audience in mind

The best storytellers customize their stories to their audience. As you would expect, that is true for a fundraising pitch too. Put yourself in the shoes of the partner you are pitching today.

In the morning, they may have had a board meeting with another portfolio company, and they may be slightly preoccupied with the challenges that came up there. They probably have two more deals they are working on at the same time, and they may have seen two other pitches already that day. There are probably three hundred emails waiting in their inbox. They walk into a room, and there you are. You've connected your laptop to the meeting room screen. They sit down. They will probably have glanced at your deck earlier in the day, and an associate may have briefed them on what your company is doing.

Before you even open your first slide, the partner will have a wall of preconceived notions about your company. Perhaps they have already looked at four companies in your space over the past couple of years. Maybe they missed out on an investment into a company founded by someone who went to the same university as you did. Perhaps they feel a fondness for you because you share a hometown or you have the same first name as their best friend. All of this is arbitrary, and none of it should have an impact on whether they invest or not. But the truth is investors are human, and they are as influenced by biases as you and me.

You have no way of knowing what biases and preconceptions your investors will bring into the room. But there are a few things you do. They are there because they are professional investors. They are there because they are looking for companies that can give them an outsize return on investment (I cover how VC works in more detail in Chapter 2).

So how does this tie into how you think about your audience? Well, for starters, it means that your investors aren't excited about the same things that excite you about the business. In the context of a slide deck, as a product-focused founder, you are probably neck-deep in three aspects of the company: who your customers are, what the problem is they are experiencing, and the solution you are building for them.

When pitching, remember that you need to keep your audience in mind. Of course, if your customers are ambivalent, the problem is nonexistent, and the product is terrible, your company will fail. And if all of those things are true, you will probably fail to raise funding.

Bear in mind that a VC firm has its business model. The limited partners (LPs—the people investing money into the venture fund) are on one side of the equation, and the startups on the other. The "problem" VCs are trying to solve is that their LPs have invested money in the venture fund, and they would like an outsize return on that investment. The "solution" they are providing is the investment thesis—the theory behind why they are investing in a particular stage and type of companies.

Of course, your startup has to fit within the investment criteria of the VC firm. If you're pitching a medical tech company to a crypto fund, that's a waste of everybody's time. Assuming you've done your research and figured out who you are pitching to, keep in mind that a product is easily amended, pivoted, or refined. The top three things investors care about are simple:

- The quality of the team (are you the right people to solve this problem?) and the ability to attract great talent (can you attract more people to help you fulfill your mission?)

- The size of the market—and whether it's growing

- The problem you are solving—and whether it's worth solving at a venture scale

This isn't to say that investors don't care at all about your product. They do. It is worth keeping in mind that when you are at the earliest stages of pitching, they only care in the context of answering the preceding questions. The product you've built to date shows how you make decisions and whether you've been able to attract early customers. It is worth pointing out that after you've raised funding, things will shift between you and the investor. The solution and the product (alongside the nebulous work of "company building") come into sharper focus.

As a founder, of course, you are passionate about the solution you are building. Your goal is to raise money, and the amount of time you have to tell the story of your company is minimal. Make it count.

Where to start your story

Your company is terrific, of course—but where do you begin telling its story? The same way you would recount a story to a friend. Start with the most significant headline. For some companies, that headline comes easily. For others, you may have to dig a little deeper. What you are optimizing for is the biggest "wow" moment—what is going to make a potential investor put their laptop aside and lean in to really pay attention to the pitch?

Remember that your story doesn't have to be chronological. If your team isn't your biggest strength, don't start with how you and your co-founders met. If your market is relatively small, don't start by laying out your total addressable market. If the problem you are solving is unsexy and "boring," but you have incredible interest from customers, you'd be crazy to start with your market.

Once you have all of your slides together, try this exercise. Think about how you would tell the story if you were to start with each of your slides. I have even seen an incredible pitch that started with an "exit" slide. Of course, the founder had an unusual story there. "I left Facebook to start my company, and within 8 months, Facebook tried to buy my company. I said 'no,' and let me tell you why…" That is storytelling.

"I have a PhD in this field and am the world's foremost expert on this type of medical procedure. There may be two people in the world who understand all of this—and I recruited the other one to be my co-founder." That is storytelling.

"There are only two ways to solve this problem. And I hold patents for both. I am building one of the solutions, and if someone else is trying to launch the other solution, they will have to licence the technology from us." That is storytelling.

"We can save each customer $10,000 per year, and our product will cost them $30 per user per year. It's a no-brainer, and we have 3,000 companies on the wait-list already—we can't make the products fast enough." That is storytelling.

You should be able to find something that makes the listener go "wow." Find out how to tell that part of the story in a compelling way. Use that to pique the interest of your listeners.

I occasionally work with founders who say, "I can't think of anything that makes investors go 'wow'." Usually, that is a sign. They may be too close to the business. They might be too modest. Or, in some cases, it's a sign that the founders should stop work on this business and go do something else instead. If there's nothing about your business that makes an investor lean forward with dollar signs in their eyes, you're going to have a really tough time raising money.

How Venture Capital Works

To raise money, you need to know what happens in the mind of a venture capitalist

In the previous chapter, I talked about why it is so important to keep your audience in mind when you are telling a story. In my work with founders, I'm sometimes surprised that even pretty experienced founders occasionally don't understand how venture capital works. By extension, it's hard to make the most compelling pitch; without understanding venture capital, it is tricky to know what the driving forces behind your investors' decisions are.

Who invests in venture capital?

At the most basic level of abstraction, venture capital (VC) is a financial asset class. Think of an "asset class" as a place where you park your money when you're not using it. As an individual, you may put your savings in a bank account, the stock market, bonds, or an index fund. You could also invest your savings in property, art, or what have you. As a smart investor, you will probably spread your risk a little. You might make some high-risk investments (say, in the stock market) that may double your money, but that could also go to zero, and you could put some of your money in government bonds or a savings account in a bank.

© Haje Jan Kamps 2020
H. J. Kamps, *Pitch Perfect*, https://doi.org/10.1007/978-1-4842-6065-4_2

The same basic principle applies to the people who invest in venture capital funds. They might be high-net-worth individuals, pension funds, university endowments, corporations, or even governments. In venture capital parlance, investors into a fund are usually called limited partners—or LPs.

Much like you, these LPs will have a "risk profile," depending on the goals they want to accomplish. A university endowment fund might be more risk averse than a high-net individual, for example. In any case, most investors will invest some of their money in low-risk investments that have a low rate of return, just above inflation. In addition, they will attempt to grow their fund, typically by allocating a small proportion of their total assets under management (AUM) to high-risk investments across various asset classes. The difference between conservative and aggressive funds is the proportion of each. For the high-risk, high-reward allocation, they may invest in private equity, which buys, optimizes, and sells existing businesses. They may choose to invest in high-risk emerging market stocks. Or perhaps they decide to invest in another high-risk asset: startups.

When an LP decides to earmark some of its money to startups, they typically don't have the expertise or the bandwidth to vet and invest in the startups directly. Instead, they deploy the funds into a company—usually a partnership—that can keep an eye out for great investment opportunities, and make the investments. These partnerships—you guessed it—are venture capital firms.

From the LPs' point of view, they hope that when they invest $10m into a VC fund, one of the investments done out of that fund is the next Facebook, Google, Tesla, or Instagram. If the fund had invested in one of those companies, $10m could turn into $200m. The startup makes a ton of cash. The VC makes a bunch of money. And the LPs stand to get an extraordinary return on their investments.

What's an investment thesis?

When talking to VCs, you need to know what the firm does and doesn't invest in. That's known as the fund's "thesis."

When people get together and establish a venture capital firm, they become the general partners (GPs) of the firm. The GPs usually invest some of their own money into the fund, but the critical part of their job is to be the legal, moral, and fiduciary shepherds of the LPs' money.

The general partners will do a lot of research and create an "investment thesis," a document that describes how the partnership will invest. The thesis will explain what the VC firm believes is going to happen over the next decade and why it has a fighting chance at giving the limited partners the return they so desire.

You may have heard of "series A" or "seed" funding rounds—usually referred to as the "stage" of the venture funding. The thesis includes the stage where the fund focuses its attention. Some firms focus on startups that don't have a product or revenue yet (sometimes referred to as pre-seed startups). Other firms will only invest in companies that already have a tremendous amount of money coming in. From an investment point of view, investing earlier is higher risk, but it's possible to get a more significant piece of the company for less money.

Some investors focus on particular markets; you'll find VC firms that only invest in virtual reality startups, hardware startups, cryptocurrency startups, medical technology, or self-driving technology startups. Other VCs focus geographically, only investing in sub-Saharan Africa, for example. Some will only invest in startups that spin out of a particular university. Some VCs decide to only invest in women, underrepresented founders, or any number of other investment criteria.

Venture capital firms can be extraordinarily broad ("we invest in all early-stage companies"). It can also be spectacularly narrow ("we only invest $20m or more into hardware companies that are working to combat cancer on the east coast of the United States and only into founders who have PhDs in related fields from a specific university"). There's no "wrong" thesis for a VC firm, as long as it can find LPs who believe in their vision.

All of these selection criteria will, together, make up the investment thesis. That is important because all of these things will be on your investor's mind. There are exceptions, of course, but as a general rule, if what you're pitching doesn't fit into the thesis, it doesn't matter how good your pitch is. The LPs won't be happy if they invested in a fighting-cancer investment prospect, and the venture firm turns around and invests in a dog-walking app aimed at millennials.

It is worth noting that most VC funds have some leeway, and there's no investor who won't at least take a look at an incredible, out-of-the-ordinary deal. This is how you sometimes see later-stage funds investing in early-stage startups, or you might experience that specialized funds make investments outside of their core thesis. Exactly how and when this happens could be a whole book all to itself, but the short version is that a lot of investors can be opportunistic, and if an incredible opportunity comes along, they may choose to pick an argument with their limited partners for the right deal.

Not all VCs will be fully open with you what their thesis is—or who their LPs are—but I wouldn't talk to a VC firm myself without researching the former and asking about the latter. You may not get an answer, but asking the question shows that you understand what's going on.

What is an exit?

A venture fund gives the company money in exchange for shares in the company. Once the investment is made, it means that the money is "locked up," and it doesn't free up again until there is a liquidity event—also known as an exit. Exits can play out a few different ways, but the two most obvious exits are an acquisition or initial public offering (IPO).

Acquisitions happen when other companies buy a startup. They do that for a few reasons; perhaps the startup has technology that the more prominent company doesn't have. Maybe they have a customer base that is hard to replicate. Maybe the startup is bought because they've built an incredible brand or perhaps the acquiring company wants to buy the startup just for its team. The latter is usually known as an "acquihire"—short for "acquisition hire"—instead of trying to hire a group of outstanding people individually, a big company might swoop in and buy the whole company. In any case, the company buys all the shares of the company, and the VC gets a payout based on how many stocks in the company they own.

The other exit is a listing on a stock exchange, usually through an initial public offering. In this scenario, the company stops being a private company and instead makes its shares available on a stock exchange. That makes the shares "liquid"—and the VC firm can sell them to stock traders who want to invest in the future of the firm.

If a company doesn't have an exit, the VCs (and, usually, the founders and staff who own shares or options in the company) won't see a payout.

How does a VC firm make money?

Most venture capital firms are set up with a "management fee" and a "carried interest" (usually just called a "carry"). The management fee tends to be 2% of the assets under management per year for the duration of the fund. So, if the fund is $100m and deployed over 6 years, the venture capital firm gets $100m × 2% × 6 years = $2m per year, for a total of $12m throughout the fund. The management fee covers the expenses, such as the wages for the staff, legal, accounting, office, travel, and other costs.

San Francisco—and the wider Bay Area—is particularly well-known for venture capital. Don't be fooled; angel investors and venture capital funds are everywhere, not just in the area south of San Francisco known as "Silicon Valley."

Much more important than the management fees, however, is the "carry." This is the cut—usually 20%—of the returns the VC fund gets for deploying the money. Exactly how the carry for the fund works varies a little, but to understand how it works, this simplified explanation works: Imagine the VC firm invests $100m into 50 startups. Some of them fail and make no return. Some return the money (i.e., the VC firm invested $2m and gets $2m back when the company "exits" some years later) or come with a modest return (say, a $3m return on a $2m investment). However, in this fund, the VC was able to invest in a startup that went on to get a huge initial public offering (IPO) on Wall Street. That $2m investment turned into $200m, and across the whole portfolio of investments, the $100m fund returned $400m. From those $400m, the venture firm gets a 20% cut or $80m. This money is divided up among the general partners. Sometimes other staff at the venture firm have some carry as well, which means they also share in those spoils.

All of which is to say, running a venture firm for $2m per year isn't particularly lucrative. General partners at venture firms are often pretty wealthy already, and they wouldn't get out of bed for the wages they are paying themselves—if any. Where things get interesting is in the carried interest, that's where a venture firm makes its real money.

What does the VC need from its investments?

Investing in startups is risky business. The exact benchmarks will depend on the stage and market the VC is investing in, but it isn't uncommon to have half of the investments fail to make a meaningful impact on the firm's financial health.

As a startup, your company failing is a terrible ordeal, but from the VC's perspective, that doesn't matter: they didn't take all their money and put it in your company—they have a whole portfolio of investments. Knowing that a lot of the investments will fail is a part of the model.

The result of all this is crucial to understand. You know that the LPs want to see a return on their investment. You also know that a lot of startups fail. The final piece of the puzzle is that if the VC firm wants to raise another fund, they need to get a decent return on the fund. So, if the VC fund wants to get a 3x return across the whole fund, it cannot invest in a company that can, at best, get a 3x return. In other words, if there is no universe where your company can result in a 10x return, it doesn't make sense for the VC to invest in your company. The big "hits" have to make up for the failures elsewhere in the portfolio.

Should you raise venture capital at all?

You picked up this book because you are interested in raising money for your company. I also feel that I should point out that venture isn't the only way to run a company.

There are downsides to venture capital-fueled companies—they run at breakneck speed, not least because the investors want to see a return on their investment, typically in a 7–10-year time horizon. Being on the VC treadmill also means that you'll continue to raise money every 12–18 months until your company either becomes self-sustaining or has an exit. Both the pace and the 7–10-year timeline may be deal-breakers for some startups; in some industries, that's not enough time to build a robust and sustainable company. And some founding teams prefer a slower, more measured approach than the breakneck venture speed affords.

If venture isn't the right path for you, it's possible to "bootstrap" your company. Find a way to get started, optimize for early revenue, and then use the income to reinvest and grow the company. Other avenues may be to seek grants or donations or raise money from angels or special-interest organizations that don't have the return expectations or time constraints inherent in a lot of venture capital models. Once you have some revenue and a clear path to more, banks and other funding sources may become options for further building and developing the business.

Pitch Deck Design

Design is important—but content is king

Many founders make the mistake of thinking that creating the pitch deck is the same as creating the pitch itself. That isn't the case on multiple levels. The "pitch" is about the story you are telling your investors. It is the answer to the question, "Why should I give you \$3m to continue building your business?" The deck helps tell part of that story, but it isn't the story itself. Crucially, you should be able to do your pitch to a VC firm without a pitch as a crutch.

Is design important?

A lot of my clients come to me and ask if I can help them with the graphical design of a pitch deck. The answer is "no"—you don't want me anywhere near the crayons. At least, not if you wish to have a beautiful pitch deck. Lack of design skills aside, the importance of the design of pitch decks is often vastly overstated.

Think about your business as a whole—is design important? In the abstract, yes—there is no excuse for actively bad design, ever. But if you use a good pitch deck template, it's pretty hard to have an aggressively lousy design. It doesn't matter if you choose to use Keynote, PowerPoint, Google Slides, or

© Haje Jan Kamps 2020
H. J. Kamps, *Pitch Perfect*, https://doi.org/10.1007/978-1-4842-6065-4_3

any of the other tools out there; there are thousands of great pitch templates. Do some research, and find something that looks good to you. Is it possible that you end up pitching with a design that someone else has used to pitch your VCs? Sure. Does it matter? Probably not.

A pitch deck is all about conveying information. I've seen a bunch of extraordinarily effective pitches that had an extremely minimal design. I've also seen some rotten pitches where the pitch deck design was exquisite.

See Figures 3-1 and 3-2, for example. This is a (fictional) high-altitude drone company selling drones for telecoms and military use. It's fair to assume that each drone costs in the millions of dollars and that the customers are large corporations and governments. In other words, while design is always important, this isn't a company like Dyson or BMW, selling its products to design-conscious consumers. As a startup founder, you're at choice for what you want as the design aesthetic for your pitch deck—but as an investor, I wouldn't judge you for choosing not to spend resources on exquisite design.

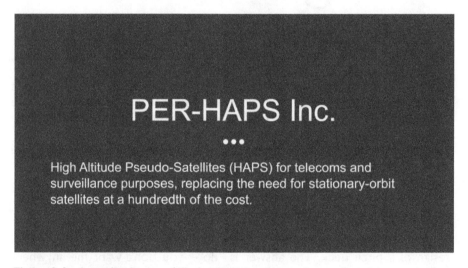

Figure 3-1. A simple, clean, no-frills design can work great. It gets the point across without distracting the viewer

Figure 3-2. A more visual approach can work well, too—as long as it helps tell part of the story. Image Source: sommersby/stock.adobe.com

Whether or not you invest in design at all depends on the kind of company you are running. If you are trying to raise money for a high-end consumer fashion brand or a luxury home automation brand aimed at consumers, your design had better be awesome. In those examples, great design is going to be an essential factor of whether or not your company is going to be successful. Lead with your strengths; make sure your pitch deck looks beautiful. If you are doing something more behind the scenes, the chances are that design plays a less important role in your business as a whole. Here are a couple of examples: Perhaps your company manufactures specialized computer chips for sub-sea cables, or you are creating a new type of insulation for industrial use. It would be prudent to invest in engineering rather than beautiful design in those cases, and nobody would hold it against you if your pitch deck were more straightforward.

If your company has a graphic designer as one of its first hires, you should probably have a beautiful pitch deck. If you do have access to design resources, you may as well use them. More importantly, the fact that you hired a designer in the first place indicates that design is a crucial aspect of your business, and it means it's probably worth investing a bit of extra care and attention to the design aesthetic of the deck.

I should point out as well that deck design can be a pretty different discipline than many other forms of design. With my clients, I have seen deck design cause friction. A founder might assign the design to a skilled designer with little or no experience in this field. I encourage you to leave your designer the space to say "no" or to work with an external resource if they need to.

The other thing to keep in mind is that the design of everything you do should be stage appropriate. There is a considerable difference between if you are two people operating out of a co-working space, trying to scrape together a $250k pre-seed round, and if you are a 300-person company raising an $80m series B.

If you don't have design resources in-house, I wouldn't invest a lot in getting someone to design a beautiful deck. Why? Because investors aren't stupid, and a well-designed presentation can be a contraindicator. In my experience, an extraordinarily beautiful pitch deck often tries to "hide" that there are holes in the business model or the pitch itself. Put differently, investors will gladly suffer a mediocre deck design that tells a fantastic story of a compelling startup. They won't be fooled by a beautiful deck where the content (i.e., the business itself, or aspects of the company) is terrible.

What are the critical design points?

The basics of good deck design are pretty simple: Use simple colors. If you include photography, make sure they are of high quality. Avoid stock photography if you can—or if you have to use it, try to find photos that don't look like they came straight out of a library. Eyeem.com is an excellent option for this; it means you can access a substantial Instagram-like library of "real" photography from talented photographers.

Use consistent fonts and font sizes—and bear in mind that you are probably tempted to include too much text on the slides. In Chapter 17, we will talk about the difference between a send-ahead deck and a presentation deck—know that there can be a lot of difference between the two.

As a rule of thumb, most slides should have fewer than 30 or so words on them. Make sure that the fonts are large—readable from across the room without squinting. In general, that means that if you have font sizes smaller than 30 points on your slide, think hard about whether that makes sense.

If you are creating a product, make sure you include recent product photography. If you're making a SaaS product, include screenshots. Think carefully about how you present graphs and figures, too—when you are busy pitching, the investors will be studying the graphs, not listen to your pitch.

Tip If you are going to include screenshots in your pitch, try to show them in context—on a computer, phone, or tablet, in the way the end user will be using them. These types of screenshots take a bit more time to produce, but it helps things come to live much better.

Should you include "builds"?

A novice mistake I see a lot is very complicated slide decks, where every slide has a lot of different "builds" or "reveals" in it. That makes sense when you are doing a keynote; being able to reveal content as you tell your story is helpful. In a pitch, however, that doesn't really work.

Think about how you are using your pitch deck; it's not a keynote. Your presentation is a conversation. I've never seen a pitch where a founder didn't flick back and forth between slides regularly, to go back to a chart or graph, or to point out a detail of the product, or to flick to the appendix to tell an auxiliary part of the story. If your slide deck is 20 slides long, you are only ever 19 clicks away from the slide you are looking for. Complicated builds mean that you may have to click "next" dozens, if not hundreds, of times. That's extremely stressful, and it gets in the way of having a good conversation. In short, don't.

How to begin, and how to close

You should probably have an opening slide that summarizes everything you do in a simple sentence. This can be your slogan or perhaps a summary of what you do. "Uber for dog-walking," (Wag) "Apple for home security," (SimpliSafe), or even "Amazon for art" (Etsy) works great—it helps level set the pitch the investors are about to hear and is a good starting point.

Figure 3-3. A closing slide or "any questions" slide is helpful, because your investors are probably going to be staring at it for a while as the discussion continues. Image Source: Fxquadro/stock.adobe.com

Make sure you have a final slide, too (Figure 3-3). It can be as simple as "Thank you" or "Any Questions?" with your contact details on it. The purpose of this slide is to make sure your investors aren't looking at your final slide when they are thinking of what they are asking questions about. As we will talk about later in this book, your first slides will be your strong points. The corollary is that your final slides will be weaker. If your very last slide, which is your go-to-market slide, is weak, and it's what is in front of people's faces as they are asking questions, guess what, you're going to get grilled on!

What Slides Will You Need?

Not all pitches need all slides to tell the full story

Slides are designed to convey a large amount of information in a short amount of time. The best way to think of the slides is as waymarkers toward how you are telling your story. Each slide is a topic, and you need to hit specific issues for your account to be complete. In later chapters of the book, I'll talk through each item you need to cover in your presentation in more detail; in this chapter, I want to talk a little about what an investor needs to know and how you organize that story.

What are the slides you need in a fundraising pitch?

Most pitches follow roughly the same order. No rule says you have to include everything. You don't even have to have them in any particular order. The following overview is a pretty good starting point for figuring out your narrative.

For some stories, you can combine several points onto the same slide or part of the story, but in general, these are the points you should try to hit.

© Haje Jan Kamps 2020
H. J. Kamps, *Pitch Perfect*, https://doi.org/10.1007/978-1-4842-6065-4_4

The problem – On the problem slide, you will explain what the problem is, why it is a problem, and who is experiencing this problem. Don't assume that the audience knows your industry. For some companies, the "problem" describes a specific pain point, such as "Taxes are too difficult to understand," "Athletes are struggling to measure their performance," or "Credit card fraud has gotten out of hand." For other companies, the "problem" is more nebulous. If you are a gaming or entertainment company, the "problem" you are solving is boredom or a desire to be entertained.

The solution – The next part of the story is what your solution is to the problem at hand. For some narratives, it is appropriate to talk about the product you are building here, but in my experience, talking about the solution in the abstract makes sense. For example, if the problem you are solving is that credit card fraud is rife, you could talk about your specific solution. However, you're talking about building a multibillion-dollar company, and the product you are making right now is probably only a small part of your vision. If that applies to you, the solution slide is your opportunity to talk about the full breadth of ways of solving the problem. At the end of this narrative arc, say something like, "That's our full vision, but to get our foot in the door, we are focusing on a specific part of this problem first…," which takes you to the product you are building now.

The product/service – If your "solution" story arc talks about the broad vision for your company, the "product/service" part of your pitch gets more detailed. Here, we want to learn more about what your solution does and how that benefits your customers. Two caveats here: One, your product could pivot further down the line as you learn more about the market, so don't commit too hard to this exact implementation of your product or service. Two, you are buried deep in the company, and the product is probably at the top of your mind. What interests your investor is how this is going to make money in the short, medium, and long term. It's incredibly tempting to dwell here, but my top tip is to give broad strokes—you'll get a chance to get into detail later.

Market size and trajectory – In this part of the story, you are answering two questions: how big is the market you are operating in, and is the market growing, stable, or shrinking?

Team – For early-stage companies, this is, by far, the most critical part of the story. You may convince investors that you have an excellent solution to a fundamental problem in a large, rapidly growing market. None of that matters if you don't have the chops to pull it off. Don't be shy when talking about your accomplishments and those of your team.

Traction – "Traction" in a startup context is whether your company is moving in the right direction. There are many ways of measuring progress in a startup. The best measurement would be revenue and, ideally, exponentially increasing revenue. There have been examples of companies raising money with a single slide, and it's almost always the "traction" slide. If you have been growing your revenue 15% week on week for a year straight, it doesn't matter what your business does or who is involved; you'll raise money. We will discuss traction in greater detail in Chapter 10.

Why now – If there is a timeliness to your company, include a "why now" slide. This part of the story connects the historical dots for why your company makes sense right now. Drones and VR, for example, couldn't have happened until smartphone manufacturers moved the needle for cheap, powerful, miniaturized technology. The electric scooter rental tech became possible because it suddenly became cheap to combine GPS and controller technology with electric scooters. If regulatory, macroeconomic, or technology makes your company possible now when it would have been unfeasible 6 years ago, include that in your story.

Business model – At the most basic level, the business model describes the following: How will your company generate revenue? Do you make one-off sales, or will you have ongoing subscriptions? If you have multiple sales channels, what are they, and what is the breakdown you are envisioning? Do you have a hybrid model (i.e., sell a product and a subscription)?

Pricing model – For some companies, the pricing model is so simple that you don't have to cover it separately from the business model. If you are creating hardware, or if you have significant capital expenditure per sale, it's worth breaking that down in more detail: What is the cost of goods sold (COGS)? What is your bill of materials (BOM) cost? What is your customer acquisition cost (CAC) to lifetime customer value (LTV)?

Go-to-market strategy – On this slide, explain how your customers will find you. Are you relying on advertising? Would building a sales team make sense? Are you relying on affiliate sales, influencer marketing, or content marketing? There are no wrong answers here, but including a robust go-to-market narrative shows that you know how to think about what it'll take to bring your product or service to market. In particular, you'll want to ensure you cover what the "beachhead" market is—which market will you tackle first, how will you reach them, and how will this help you unlock additional markets?

Market landscape/competitors – If you've found a problem worth solving, you have competitors. Maybe you don't have anyone doing the same thing you are doing, but there will be other ways of solving the same problem—explain them here and add why your solution is better—or at least different. Also, bear in mind that you will probably have some "competitive alternatives." For example, if you make dishwashing machines, other dishwasher manufacturers are direct competitors. It is also possible to wash dishes by hand, to use disposable plates, or to have a maid. Those are competitive alternatives—make sure you know what they are and how they impact your business.

The moat – This chapter is named after the water feature you find around castles to keep intruders out. In the context of a startup, well, it means the same thing: do you have something that prevents your competitors from coming after you? In some companies, this might be a patent portfolio. For others, it's all about a strong, recognizable brand. For others, it may be the team, people that have skills and experience beyond any other.

The ask and use of funds – You are pitching for a reason to raise money. On this slide, you explain how much money you are attempting to raise and what milestones you'll reach with those funds.

Operating plan – For some pitches, an operating plan is a little too in the weeds. If your investors are interested, you'll need to talk about this soon enough, so you may as well include it. The operating plan consists of a high-level plan for the next 18 months or so of your company; what milestones will you hit in terms of product launches, user growth, hiring goals, and other metrics? Ideally, the money you ask for in your "ask" should map pretty neatly to your operating plan. If it doesn't, you'll need to be prepared to have a pretty good explanation.

Don't include an "exit strategy" slide!

The only slide I sometimes see in slide decks that is best avoided is the "exit strategy" slide. That might be counterintuitive: after all, the investors care about little else, so why wouldn't you include it? In short, it's a no-win part of the story. Remember that institutional investors do this for a living. They think about investments and the long-term plans for startups thirty times per day. It's extremely unlikely that you're able to add something to that line of thinking—they've thought of potential exits for your startup as soon as they've seen the cover slide. And more ideas will come up as you go through your pitch.

Figure 4-1. A lot of founders include an "exit strategy" slide. For many reasons, that's best avoided. Image Source: Tierney/stock.adobe.com

If you do include an exit slide (see Figure 4-1), the best-case scenario is that you'll have thought of all the same things as they have. The worst-case scenario is that you're introducing exit scenarios that don't make sense to the VC, for reasons you don't have visibility into. And now, you're on the back foot, yielding your valuable pitching time to talking about a subject you're not an expert on and that that ultimately doesn't matter.

The truth is **you don't know**. Your exit is probably 5–10 years away. In that decade, you will learn more about your market than you'll ever imagine. Competitors will appear, incumbents will shift, and whole universes (metaphorically speaking) will boil off into space.

In short, it's futile to even speculate. You are going to be wrong. And if you are somehow right—that is, you were able to call what your exit was 5 years before it happened—you were probably right for the wrong reasons; there's no extra credit for calling your shots.

The other thing to keep in mind is that exit strategy thinking sends the wrong signal: one of the ways that VCs lose money is companies exiting too early. A lot of focus on a potential exit strategy shows the investors that the founders might take a deal too early, which might make the founders wealthy but doesn't fit into the firm's investment thesis.

If you are pushed on your exit strategy in a pitch meeting, say something like "I am building a company for the ages. We are planning for an IPO in 7 years or less, and if other opportunities come up before then, we will discuss it with our board." That simple statement shows a few things: You are in it for the long haul. You're prepared to keep slogging along to build a valuable company. And you know that there's a dynamic in place: Your board (and, by extension, your investors) get a say in any exit conversations.

What order do slides go in?

In broad strokes, the content that goes into pitch decks is pretty much the same—that's the point, and it helps investors get a comprehensive overview of the company they are looking at quickly. We just covered that: what's the problem, how are you solving it, how big is the market, what's the competition, what's your team, how much money are you raising, and so on.

In working with a ton of startups as a pitching coach, I often come across an awkward problem. Many—probably most—of the people I work with found an excellent template for a pitch deck somewhere on the Internet, and incidentally, that's what I recommend you do as you're working on the deck. The problem is that if you only customize the slides without thinking about the order they are in, you'll run into issues with your story.

You don't tell your story to match your slides—you use the slide to support and enhance your account. This has a couple of benefits: If your slides don't work or you can't get the computer to connect to the screen (it happens more than you might think), you shrug, and you present without slides. More importantly, the slides shouldn't be the focus of your attention: your story is. If your Keynote or PowerPoint is stealing the show, you've already lost. The investors don't need to have faith in your presentation wizardry; they need to have confidence in you.

In other words, lead from your strength. Investors see tons of pitches every day, and the temptation is always to write you off before you've gotten started. To catch an investor's attention, your first slide should be something that surprises and delights.

If you have incredible traction, lead with a graph showing that. If you have the only team that could possibly run this company, that's your first slide. Do you have patented technology? Is the problem unusual and exciting? Is the market surprising and snowballing?

The first slide is the answer to "what's unusual about this company." From there, tell the story the way you would tell the story. A fundraising pitch isn't a linear story, so there are no rules to where you can start—as long as it supports a compelling narrative arc that you follow from beginning to end.

There's no "right" order to the slides—but there is a wrong way. If you find yourself jumping back and forth in your narrative a lot, you've found the latter.

Slide: The Problem

... And why it is worth solving

One prominent trait of an entrepreneurial person is that they see challenges all around them. Nothing is ever as easy to use, as efficient, or as smooth as it ought to be. As entrepreneurs, we go through life always thinking, "how can I make this experience better?"

Put four entrepreneurial people in a room with a whiteboard, and you can come up with 200 issues that could do with some improvement in a couple of hours. I know, because I've done this exercise several times. It's a wonderfully creative process, and it's incredible how many things in the world around us are subpar.

The reason I mention this is that ideas are cheap. Nothing is so good that it couldn't be improved. And not all problems are worth solving.

An example of a "problem" might be that people forget to take their vitamins. That feels like a real problem, but there's an issue: if you go and ask a thousand people what they would do if they forgot to take their vitamins, I predict you'll be met with a shrug most of the time. Put differently, the problem might be real, but nobody is willing to spend money to solve it.

© Haje Jan Kamps 2020
H. J. Kamps, *Pitch Perfect*, https://doi.org/10.1007/978-1-4842-6065-4_5

Another "problem" might be that elderly people are on crucial, life-saving medicines to help them breathe and keep their blood pressure regulated. Ask the same people if they would pay to ensure they take medication every day. You can see where I'm going with this.

I often talk to my clients about "vitamins" and "painkillers." Vitamins are a nice-to-haves—if you realize you're out of vitamins, you might pick some up the next time you're in the shop. And if you forget during that shopping trip, that's fine, too. Painkillers, however, are a different story. If you have a headache, you'll go out of your way to solve the problem. You might make a separate trip to the store, or you'll ask a friend to bring you some.

When you are describing your problem as part of the pitch, you must connect on an emotional level. Does this problem induce stress in people? Does it inflict emotional or physical pain? Does the issue put lives at risk, cause lost sleep, or cost tremendous amounts of money? Does it cause wasted effort, and would a solution to this problem increase the efficiency of your customers? As shown in Figure 5-1, the challenge doesn't have to be groundbreaking or dramatic; as long as people are willing to pay to solve the problem somehow, you're on your way.

Using examples when talking about a problem can be a powerful tool to make issues come to life. "Linda is in accounts payable. She spends several hours per day checking whether customers have paid their invoices. She is so busy that she's expecting she may have to hire an assistant to do her job. Sometimes, she makes mistakes and sends reminders to customers who have already paid or fails to send reminders for overdue invoices. Linda's mistakes cause unhappy customers at best or cash flow issues for the business at worst." Using narratives to bring a problem to life can help illustrate why it is so important and why the problem has a real impact on small businesses. When you get to the market slide, you can continue the story with "Remember Linda and her struggles? There are 90,000 Lindas in the United States alone."

> ## The problem: The only thing more sad than an empty fridge, is a fridge filled with uninspiring beer
>
> - People are eager to explore new beers, but there are too many choices
>
> - Shopping for beer at a liquor store or supermarket is underwhelming and confusing
>
> - Getting good advice is hard

Figure 5-1. The trick of creating a great "problem" slide is to help the investor empathize with the problem formulation. For some businesses (such as our fictional beer subscription company), that is pretty straightforward. For other businesses, it can be quite complicated. Don't assume that your investor has in-depth knowledge about the market and problem you are describing. Image Source: Lightfield Studios/stock.adobe.com

In the context of fundraising, remember that a feature is not a product. You may create a tool to help people create canned responses for their email. "Tom sends 900 emails per day, and he finds that he is often saying the same things again and again. He is copying and pasting snippets of text from a Word document he created, but that's not efficient." On the face of it, that's a real problem worth solving. But is Tom willing to pay for it? Creating it as a stand-alone company might make sense. Still, it is hard to imagine it being a billion-dollar company: if you get successful enough, other companies will launch templating systems for an email in their core offering. At that point, your business will become irrelevant overnight. To wit, Gmail has templates built in, and most customer relationship management (CRM) software has snippets and templates built in, too.

The gold standard for a problem slide describes a huge problem that many people are experiencing. Solving this problem would have an immense impact on their lives, and they are willing to pay a lot of money to make that problem go away.

Twilio is an excellent example of such a company. It made it easy for software developers to send SMS messages and to route phone calls. Before Twilio came along, if you wanted to transmit messages, you needed to buy costly servers and place them within the network of the phone operators. It takes a lot of deep expertise and incredible expense to do that right. God forbid you'd need to send SMS in many different countries; you'd have to build a specialized telecoms team in each nation you are operating. For a company like Uber, their core competency is to create apps for passengers and drivers, deal with payments, and route passengers the most efficient way possible. Dealing with the minutia of sending messages and routing calls is a waste of their time, and they are delighted to outsource it. The pain point Twilio solves, then, is that for software developers, dealing with the peculiarities and cost of telecoms networks is a pain and a huge distraction.

When telling the story of the problem, it's helpful to have some examples of how people are currently solving the problem. "Company X had to hire four full-time staff and buy $50,000 of telecoms equipment to set up their SMS infrastructure" is a great way to bring Twilio to life. "For your webshop, the running of server hardware is painful and unpredictable. If you have a sudden spike in traffic, it can take weeks to get extra capacity, and you might lose millions of dollars as the web pages are unavailable" is a compelling argument for Amazon Web Services (AWS). "Linda needs to hire an assistant to deal with her workload" is an excellent argument for automatic account reconciliation and reminder-sending software solutions.

Your job as the founder is to draw a solid, realistic picture of the problem you're about to solve, explain the pressing need people have for addressing the issue, and give an indication of how prevalent the problem is. Also, include the risks or costs of what happens if the question remains unsolved. If your "problem" slides tick all of those boxes, you're on the right path.

Slide: The Solution

… And how you are different from other solutions on the market

Once you've convinced your would-be investor that the problem you're tackling is worth solving, the obvious next step is how you're going to solve that problem.

In this book, I handle "the solution" and "the produc" in different chapters. They are very closely related, and many founders can safely combine both into either a "product" or a "solution" slide. Conceptually, however, I think they are a little different.

When you are pitching your company to an investor, you are telling two stories in parallel. One version is the ultimate vision you have for your company. To use Uber as an example, they started off wanting to disrupt the taxi market, with town cars that come to your house, summoned by an app. That was a big vision, of course, but at some point, they shifted toward wanting to be the hub for all gig-economy transport needs. They launched Uber Eats for food delivery, Uber Freight for substantial transportation needs, and Uber Business to make it easy for businesses to transport their staff and customers around. The "solution," in the context of the pitch deck, is the full vision for your company.

© Haje Jan Kamps 2020

H. J. Kamps, *Pitch Perfect*, https://doi.org/10.1007/978-1-4842-6065-4_6

When talking about the solution, you have some wiggle room to talk about the broader problem and how it fits into the context of the customers and how you envision a suite of products that can help customers. Airbnb started as "Airbed and Breakfast," but it is now a vast marketplace economy offering lodging, experiences, and more. The broader vision of Airbnb stemmed from starting the lodging business and then discovering that there were many other pain points in the travel industry. If you were pitching Airbnb today, you could envision it as a one-stop travel planning website. Plan your trip, the things you do, the places you eat, and more.

When thinking about the solution you are presenting, think about the big, 10-year vision for your company. In your big-picture plan, you have an opportunity to show off how deeply you understand the market you are entering and the challenges your customers are facing. You can hint at a suite of products, several services, or a platform that becomes the go-to place for your customers to solve more and more problems in your space. By painting the solutions in broad strokes, you have a chance to put some meat on the dream you're selling. The investor wants to know that you have an expansive idea and that your company won't be a one-trick pony. Ultimately, there has to be a path for your enterprise to become a multibillion-dollar company, showing that you have the knowledge and ambition to get there which is of great help.

Apple started with the Apple I, a computer for hobbyists. Sony's first product was a (mostly unsuccessful) rice cooker. Amazon started as an online bookstore. Google's parent company Alphabet started as just a search engine. All of these companies came from humble beginnings, and most of them weren't even the first company of its kind. But the founders were visionaries who realized that there were vast industries worth conquering. The trick to describing the "solution" part of your deck, then, is to put some meat behind your vision. How are you going to change the world?

A word of warning. Your investors will want to see that you have a vision for how to move the universe, of course, but they also want to be reassured that you know how to stay focused. As seen in Figure 6-1, make sure you have a clearly articulated vision for what your solution covers.

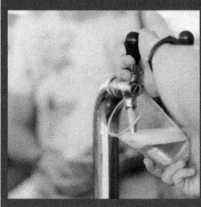

Figure 6-1. For BeerSub.com, we could probably have combined the "solution" and "product" slides—but compare this slide with the one in Chapter 7 to see how they tell a slightly different part of the story. Image Source: Максим Коробский/stock.adobe.com

A crucial piece of painting the "big picture" is to reassure your audience that you won't be trying to take it all on at once. Once you've explained your long-term vision, outline where you're going to start; what is the first piece you'll bite off? If you are using a single slide for the "solution," make sure you include where you are focusing your attention at first. If you're doing a solution and a product slide separately, make sure you highlight that the long-term vision is viable only once you've gotten a foothold on the market. Then explain what that foothold is going to be.

Slide: The Product

What does the solution actually do?

In the previous chapter, we talked about the solution and how you're painting a broad-view image of how your company is going to address the problem you've identified in the market. As we discussed, for some presentations, the solution is the same as the product, but I like to think of them as slightly different slices of the same pie. Whereas the "solution" is a broader vision for the problem space, the "product" is more specific; it speaks to the product or solution you are planning to present to your customers first.

When telling your product story, it's crucial to keep in mind that—as with any business—your product might change over time. Or, put differently, your broader "solution" is the fabric of your business; it probably won't change drastically over the lifetime of your company. Your product, however, is your current stab at how you're going to present your solution to the world. Over the lifetime of your company, you will probably have a suite of products that are taking on the problem you are trying to solve.

To bring that into context, let me use the Microsoft Office suite as an example. The problem Office is solving is that businesses need to be able to make presentations (PowerPoint), keep track of their finances (Excel), and create documents (Word). The overall "solution" that Microsoft was offering in this

© Haje Jan Kamps 2020

H. J. Kamps, *Pitch Perfect*, https://doi.org/10.1007/978-1-4842-6065-4_7

space was ways of making your business better and easier to use. Over the years, the Office suite has contained several products that were since retired. Microsoft Encarta was an encyclopedia, Microsoft Money was a personal finance tracking software package, and Microsoft Schedule was an application for scheduling, for example. Overall, the problem Office kept solving was consistent ("Make life easier for office workers"), but the products that were part of the suite kept evolving—and whole product lines were added, and discontinued, to stay on mission.

For a startup, it would be unwise to go after the entire Office suite as a whole. Microsoft has a tremendous foothold in that universe. It is unlikely that you'll be able to offer an end-to-end solution that is better than what Microsoft is offering. However, it isn't unthinkable that you might be able to come up with a product that is an excellent competitor to one of the apps in the Office suite. Airtable, for example, can be used as a spreadsheet—but it adds incredibly powerful functionality that makes it much better than Excel for specific use cases. There are a ton of alternatives to PowerPoint for presentations. And while my publisher, Apress, wants my manuscript as a Word document, I am writing this book in Grammarly (see Grammarly.com), because I enjoy the real-time spellcheck and grammar advice far better than Microsoft Word can offer.

Think of your "solution" slide as the Microsoft Office of your market. What suite of products can you offer to help solve several problems for your customers? That's your longer-term goal. For your product slide, you are describing the "thin edge of the wedge." What product do you need to offer to your customers to provide real value and get your foot in the door?

I recommend that my clients start the narrative with the solution. Imagining for a moment that MS Office didn't exist, the solution pitch might be this: "In the office software space, customers have a wide span of needs. There is an opportunity for creating a suite of closely interlinked products that help office workers be more productive." From there, you can tackle the product. "In time, we plan to address the full breadth of customer needs. We are starting by tackling the most important problem; accountants need to tabulate budgets manually. We can save them hundreds of hours and a huge amount of unnecessary mistakes."

Figure 7-1. In your "product" slide, you have a chance to talk about what your product does. Try to keep it benefits driven, rather than feature driven. Investors care more about how the product makes your customers' lives better, than the specifics of how it achieves that goal. Image Source: Yummy pic/stock.adobe.com

By structuring the narrative this way, you can help your potential investors buy into your big-picture vision and take a more detail-oriented approach next. This has two advantages: for one, if they get the big idea for what you are trying to do, you're laying the groundwork for them dreaming big about your potential exit and, in turn, their fund-returning payday. It also helps contextualize what you are hoping to accomplish and aids in showing that you are the kind of founder who can think both at the macro- and microlevel. The second significant advantage is that even if they don't fully agree with how you are tackling the market first—say, that you are trying to take on Office by tackling Excel first, but they would prefer you overthrow Word first—they can see the direction you are going. If you can make a compelling case for your first product and how it is of strategic importance for the second phase of your product rollout, it shows that you can think about a product road map dynamically.

Whatever you do, don't pitch a full suite of products to early-stage investors. Even if the products are tightly integrated, it is usually better to bring one product to market first and learn from the launch and customer feedback before you launch your second product. In our BeerSub.com example (see Figure 7-1), we are starting by tackling a pretty simple slice of the market; you could imagine that the company will continue to grow into other market segments (wine, kombucha, perhaps even soft drinks) that can dispense out of the same taps. But starting with just beer is an easy way to test the market.

I see a lot of pitches where startups are planning to launch two, three, or sometimes even more products at once. The risk is too high. In the history of startups, there hasn't been a product that found the perfect product/market fit from its launch; there are always learnings and adjustments that need to happen to find your stride. One of the advantages of being a founder is being nimble—you may as well keep that advantage for as long as you can.

A common mistake is to get the audience wrong for your product slide. By now, you're probably used to selling your product to your customers. It is natural to have a temptation to pitch your product slide as if your investors are potential buyers. That doesn't work: your investors don't inherently care about your product, and even if they are personally interested in buying it, the investor deck is not the right place to do that. The "product" the investors are "buying" is ownership in your company, not the products or solutions you sell. Instead, think of your product slide as a compelling reason to invest. The product slide, then, should bolster the argument for investing, not sell the product itself. Tell the story of how your product fits into the overall solution. Explain how the product is an excellent fit for customers. Contextualize that with the market dynamics in your industry.

As a founder, you spend a lot of your time creating compelling products. You are rightfully proud of the work your company has done to date, and your milestones are worth celebrating. It may be tempting to lead with your product slide to tell the story of your company, but that's almost always the wrong decision. If you have traction, that's a better slide to lead with—and if your product is magnificent, contextualize it with your bigger vision (the "solution" slide), rather than waxing lyrical about the product itself.

Slide: Market

Where is the market today? Where is it going?

Given that you now understand how venture capital works (Chapter 2), you'll have figured out that it's unlikely you'll find a venture-backable business in a small market. In other words, it doesn't matter if you have 100% of the market share for corrective eye surgery for left-handed pet ferrets. The market is not going to be big enough to build a billion-dollar business, which means it's going to be tremendously hard to raise venture capital.

Three essential things go into your market size slide, and it's important you think about all of them. The first element is the overall market size—that is, how valuable is the entire annual market. The next part is the market trajectory; is the market growing? If so, how quickly? Finally, you wouldn't be able to take 100% of the market, so the question is what proportion of the market your company could reliably address?

Let's take a closer look at all of those in order.

Market size

You can determine the market size in many different ways, and there is no objectively wrong way of looking at it. You will want to take a contextual approach; if you are fundraising to launch in the US market, it is less relevant to talk about the global market size. If you are planning to do a regional launch, it would be natural to include both national and local market sizing.

© Haje Jan Kamps 2020
H. J. Kamps, *Pitch Perfect*, https://doi.org/10.1007/978-1-4842-6065-4_8

Determining the size of a market is a mixture of art and science, and the part that is science isn't particularly accurate. That is okay; what the investors will be looking for is whether you have a firm grasp of what the market dynamics are in your space and whether you have a realistic way of reaching your customers.

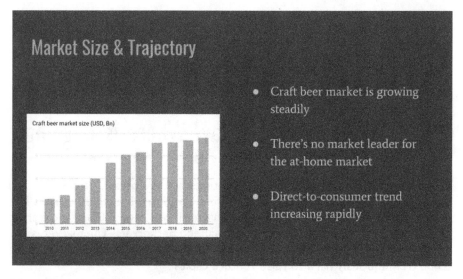

Figure 8-1. However you size your market, it's important to illustrate that if you're able to take a meaningful market share, it's worth taking a bet on you. As an investor, this slide would give me pause: it looks like the market has flattened out over the last few years. That might indicate that the market is maturing and that it is harder to get a foothold. If that is the case, make sure you have a good story ready for how you're going to gain market share from the incumbents!

A great starting point for market sizing is a simple Google search; if an extensive, established consulting firm has written a white paper or published a report about your market or industry, you'll want to know about it. Two reasons: One, that is the number your VCs will find when they are doing their due diligence; if your figures are significantly different, you should be prepared to defend your numbers. The other reason is that market analysts have a much deeper reach and usually a pretty good grasp of the markets where they have expertise. Are they going to be exactly correct? Probably not, but then, neither will you.

If you can't find published research about market sizing, you'll have to make your approximations. At its simples, if there are 100,000 businesses buying widgets in the United States, and they, on average, purchase $500 worth of widgets, that means that the market size is $50m per year. You'll have to be prepared to defend both figures: How do you know that there are that many businesses buying widgets? How do you know that the average spend is $300? A lot of the time, both these figures will represent educated guesses, and that's okay—as long as you end up roughly in the right order of magnitude for the annual market size.

Market trajectory

Market trajectories are hugely important in deciding whether to invest in a particular market. In a past life, I ran a startup that was serving the digital photography world. The problem, of course, was that smartphones were on the rapid rise, and compact camera sales went off a cliff. In just 5 years, the number of stand-alone digital camera sales plummeted by 90%. That's not pretty, and investors were rightly dubious about the entire market as a result.

The opposite is also true: "A rising tide raises all boats" is a saying that continues to ring true for many investors. Put differently, if you can grab a 30% market share in a small market, and then the market itself grows exponentially, the dynamic of your company is going to be interesting. You don't have to increase your market share: you can have a rapidly growing business by just "riding the wave" as it develops. Spotify is an excellent example of this; when the founders started the company in 2006, CDs were already in sharp decline. By launching one of the first legal competitors to the Kazaas and the Napsters of the world, Spotify was able to take, and hold, a large share of the market.

In the market trajectory portion of your pitch, you have a chance to shine. Not only do you get to show off that you have a deep understanding of your market, but you can also bring in the macroeconomic trends that affect the business you are conjuring into being. Again, be prepared to defend why the market is growing. You should be able to explain both what is happening in your markets and why.

Addressable market

You may have heard of "TAM, SAM, SOM"—or total addressable market, serviceable available market, and serviceable obtainable market. A lot of founders choose to include all three numbers on the market slide because they all tell a slightly different part of the story.

Your TAM should be the same as "market size," discussed earlier. It describes the total demand for a product in the market. If you are to launch a new type of toothpaste, for example, you'd find out what the value is of all the toothpaste sold in the United States.

Note   One quick heads-up here. If you are in a marketplace economy, you want to capture just the value of the actual marketplace, not of the economy as a whole. In other words, if you are launching a competitor to eBay, you don't want the value of all the transactions that happen on eBay; you'll want the size of the commission that eBay charges.

Your SAM—serviceable available market—carves out the part of the market that you can meaningfully address. Your SAM recognizes that even though the whole market for toothpaste might be huge, you cannot compete at all fronts. Perhaps you start with just a tooth-whitening toothpaste or just a travel-size toothpaste. The SAM will be smaller than the TAM because you are excluding yourself from dentist-prescribed kinds of toothpaste or other specialty toothpastes.

Finally, your SOM is the portion of the SOM that you think you can capture. Even if you decide to focus on tooth-whitening toothpaste, you are unlikely to win 100% of the market—incumbents like Aquafresh and Colgate are never going to go away completely. The number you are looking for here is what you can achieve.

How to tell the story of your market

For your market size slide, it is often tempting to tell the story through numbers. That can work, but it's tough to spin a compelling narrative yarn there. Use the TAM/SAM/SOM numbers to tell a story that brings the numbers to life. This is easiest if you refer back to examples you've used earlier in your pitch:

"Remember Lisa, the person who was struggling to remember to buy toothpaste?" you can start the callback. "It turns out that there are 40 million Lisas in the US alone, and we think we can convince a third of them to sign up for our toothpaste subscription. From there, as we launch additional product lines, the serviceable market just grows."

Slide: Team

Why you are the right people to solve this problem

In the world of early-stage startups, your team is the most valuable asset you have. It doesn't matter if you're in the world's sexiest market with the freshest product on the block. Ultimately, your investors are investing in you and your team. When they are considering whether to invest or not, the main question they are asking themselves is whether the people at the top of the food chain at your company have what it takes to walk the perilous and meandering path of startups. The way you tell the story of your team is crucial. It will mean the difference between raising money and not raising money.

Every day of the week, a venture capitalist will sit in a meeting room and see pitches from some of the best people in the world at what they do—people who have perfect "founder-market fit."

To understand how to tell the story of your team, you need to know what investors look for in teams. What it boils down to is risk reduction. Startup teams—and in particular, the founding teams—have several skills and attributes. Some of them will go in your favor, and others will count against you. It is worth mentioning that different investors have varying opinions on what makes a good founding team. Some investors prefer to invest in teams that have deep startup experience, while others are happy to invest in teams that are fresh out of college. It is worth doing a little bit of research before you do your pitching to see what your investors prefer.

© Haje Jan Kamps 2020
H. J. Kamps, *Pitch Perfect*, https://doi.org/10.1007/978-1-4842-6065-4_9

Attributes of winning teams

If your team has previous startup experience, it is worth highlighting that. Founders who have had multiple exits and who have made venture capital firms a lot of money in the past often have an easier time raising money than teams who have never founded a startup before.

Non-successful startups are worth mentioning, too. Even if you didn't have a massive exit, there's no shame in having started a company and failed. Remember that most VCs have invested in dozens, if not hundreds, of companies before. The model for venture capital dictates that a lot of these companies fail—and that is okay. You can learn a lot of useful things even from running a "failed" startup—I should know, most of the companies I founded turned out to be complete and utter failures, financially. The critical thing to be able to formulate is why you think the company failed. If it was the market, then you should be prepared to outline what your initial assumptions were, what changed, and what you learned. If it was your fault, take ownership and explain how you've changed so that it can't happen again.

Even if you weren't a startup founder yourself, if you were part of an early-stage (30 or fewer staff) company, you could learn a lot of the startup magic by osmosis. Weave those experiences into your team slide as well.

Have you never been at a startup? No problem—what other work experiences do you have that's relevant? What skills, knowledge, and attributes do you have that nobody else has? One example of this that comes up often is people transitioning out of academia. You may have a PhD in a particular topic, and you could be the world's foremost expert on something. That has incredible value—make sure to highlight it as part of your team narrative.

If you're starting a company in an industry you know well, make sure you emphasize that. For example, if you spent 25 years inventing new types of paint at the world's largest paint manufacturer, that is relevant if you are creating a paint startup. In Figure 9-1, I'm illustrating what an excellent team slide might look like. Note that while it's customary to have the CTO in the main slot, feel free to play around with the order of that, as long as you are able to tell a good story around it.

Figure 9-1. The team slide typically only includes the founding team for a startup; these are the people who have committed to building this company together, and the thread that will keep the company together as it grows and develops. Image Sources: [Master1305]/stock. adobe.com; [Lightfield Studios]/stock.adobe.com; [Volodymyr]/stock.adobe.com

Another angle you can take is that of the "expert customer." When I started my first company, Triggertrap, I had never done a real startup before, and I hadn't created photography equipment or a hardware product previously. But the one advantage I did have is that I had written over fifteen books about photography at that point. I was a legitimate "expert customer," which means that our company had an unfair advantage: I deeply understood the problem space I was entering into. Some of the best companies in the world are started by people who "scratch their own itch." They are the founders who experienced a problem at work or in their personal life, time and time again— and they are so tired of the issue that they are motivated to find a solution.

Why are you starting this company?

I do occasionally work with founders who have none of the above: They might have some work experience, but it isn't directly relevant to the company they are starting. They don't have patents or direct expertise in the problem space. And they aren't an "expert customer." The hardest question I ever ask a founding team is this: "So, why are you the right people to start this company right now?" It would be best if you had an excellent answer to this question— because, ultimately, everything in this chapter is about answering that exact question.

In the course of my pitch coaching, I have talked several people out of starting companies. The reason was almost always the "founder-market-fit" question. If the founder doesn't have a real, deep, reliable connection with the market, the question that won't melt away is, "why is this founder even trying to start this company?" If the founder can't come up with the right answer, there's a fundamental problem with this company. In my opinion, only one thing can help: phenomenal amounts of traction. Traction—whether that materializes as subscribers, sales, monthly active users, or what have you—proves that no matter what the founding team looks like on paper, they know how to execute and can turn into a profitable business. If you don't have a team with a strong founder-market fit, and you didn't have traction to overcome that, nobody will invest: it would simply be too high-risk a proposition.

For your team slide, at the early stages of your company, you'll want to focus on your founding team, as they are the ones who are "locked into" the business. Your broader team of staff and contractors also tell part of the story, but ultimately it is possible for them to leave; their value isn't tied to the company itself in the same way. The individual members of the junior team are generally not relevant to the pitch. It would be best if you showed the team sizes of your different teams. If you have 90% developers, 10% customer support, and zero sales or marketing people, for example, you may have some explaining to do as to how your business is growing.

As your company starts growing, your senior team is there to fill in the gaps of the founding team. Here, you will be judged on your skill in attracting, hiring, and retaining key members of your organization. This is as important as the founders themselves. As a founder, know what your shortcomings and weaknesses are. If marketing makes you cringe, surround yourself with proven marketeers. If spreadsheets make your eyes glaze over, hire a great operations person or a finance person to help cover that side of the business. The story of the team you have in place and the people you are planning to hire soon is the story of how you can build a team that can stand the test of time.

Finding the narrative

Your team should be good enough to warrant telling a story about; all you have to do is to find the narrative. Some groups I work with are so good and so impressive that I advise them to lead the whole pitch with the team slide. Others are less impressive, but they still end up successfully raising money. The main message you need to get across is why the group of people going on this adventure together has a fighting chance at building a valuable company in the market they are entering.

Slide: Traction

How are you measuring your success to date? What milestones have you hit?

"Traction," in the world of startups, is your finger on the pulse to indicate whether what you are doing is working or not working. Call them key performance indicators (KPIs), metrics, or "traction."

Throughout your company's life, the metric that matters to your startup is going to vary a lot. If you end up exiting through a stock listing (such as a direct listing or an IPO), one of the primary metrics you'll be judged on is the company's share price and the number of shares in the calculation—together expressed as the company's market capitalization (or "market cap"). Don't be fooled into thinking that metrics are only necessary for the later stages of your entrepreneurial journey. Most successful startups start tracking metrics from day one—and the development of those metrics is a crucial part of your pitch to investors.

Revenue is king

As far as metrics go, revenue is king. A startup that is generating a large amount of recurring revenue can raise money at any time, as long as they have a good story for how they are going to spend the invested capital to grow revenue further. However, if your company were throwing off huge bags of

H. J. Kamps, *Pitch Perfect*, https://doi.org/10.1007/978-1-4842-6065-4_10

cash every month, you probably wouldn't be reading this book. The obvious truth is that for a lot of startups, you're not going to be generating revenue quite yet—but metrics are no less important!

I've seen many startup founders use subjective measures, such as "product in beta" or "improved onboarding" as indicators of traction. Think about this from your investor's point of view; if there are no objective data indicating how you are doing, how can they measure how well the company is doing?

Remember also that investors rarely invest in a single data point but on trends. If your 3-month-old company has 900 customers, that's impressive, but what is even more impressive is seeing how those customers have accumulated over time.

Be aware of so-called vanity metrics. These are objective metrics that can show progress in your company, but that doesn't matter in the long run. The number of Twitter followers, number of people on your mailing list, and number of inbound inquiries are all critical metrics for the running of the business, of course. Still, your investor isn't going to care. Why? You can buy Twitter followers cheaply, you don't know the value of each of the people who subscribed to your mailing list, and it's unclear whether those inbound inquiries are going to convert into sales.

Track early, track often

There are a few metrics you should start tracking right away. Keep an eye on your cost of acquisition (CAC); this is a dollar value that explains how much money you had to spend on advertising to acquire a customer. Of course, this varies by channel. Your content marketing and public relations may turn out to be extremely cheap ways of acquiring customers, but it's hard to scale those channels by pouring more money into them. Your advertising channels (Facebook, YouTube, AdWords, eBay, Amazon, Twitter, etc.) are more expensive, but are more scalable: if a channel is proving to be successful, add more money to the budget to make more sales there. Some channels are hard to attribute (word of mouth, print, radio, or podcast advertising), but what you can know is how much money you are spending in total and how many new customers you attract. This total number of customers divided by cost is your "blended customer acquisition cost"—or blended CAC.

The other number you should know is how much a customer is worth over its lifetime—or their lifetime value (LTV). If you only ever plan to make one sale to a customer, that number is easy to know: if they spend $99 on average and never come back to spend more money, your LTV is $99. Your LTV gets more complicated if you expect customers to come back from time to time, for example, if you sell golf balls that eventually get lost, but your customers are super happy and keep buying the same balls.

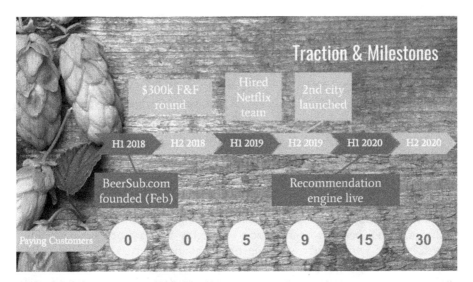

Figure 10-1. Your traction slide is an opportunity to show real, measurable progress in the history of the startup. Image Source: ruslan_khismatov/stock.adobe.com

If you run a subscription-based business, your LTV can be complicated; you don't know how long your customer will be a customer. You'll have to make assumptions on this front—and be prepared to able to explain and defend those assumptions. If you are Netflix, your customers may stay around for 4 years, on average, paying $14.99 per month. That means that the LTV of a Netflix customer is $720 or so.

If you don't have "hard" traction, it's still worth including a traction slide. Show what you've accomplished and when. Figure 10-1 shows what that could look like. In most B2C companies, 30 paying customers are nothing to shout about, but this slide lays the groundwork for telling a story of growth and ambition.

As a business, you'll want your lifetime value to go up. You'll want your cost of acquisition to go down. And, of course, you'll need your overall number of customers to grow. If you can express both your CAC and your LTV, then you can get to a ratio between the two. The benchmark here is a 3:1—in other words, you make 3x more money off a customer than it costs to acquire them. If you can do better than that, print it big on your slides—it is a great way to tell the story of your growth on your traction slide.

If you don't know what your lifetime value of a customer is going to be, there are other metrics you can use to show how your company is growing. Monthly active users (i.e., how many people are actively engaging with your app regularly) is a helpful metric to express how "sticky" your product is. Average time spent in app can indicate how much people care about your product. A net promoter score (NPS) can be an indication of how happy your customers are with the product.

▮ **Tip**   To calculate your NPS, there's plenty of calculators online, but in short, you've probably seen the question, "Would you recommend this to a friend?" The answers are fed into an algorithm of detractors (people who voted 0-6), promoters (9s and 10s). The percentage of your promoters less the percentage of your detractors is your net promoter score. Your NPS can range from minus 100 to positive 100—so a NPS of 60 is much better than it might look.

If you are pre-launch, you may not have meaningful metrics to share, which is a shame. You'll have no ammunition to deploy to convince your would-be investors that what you're working on is gaining traction. If that describes your situation, you may end up with metrics that are less objective and, instead, express your traction as "milestones to date." Most of these metrics will be subjective, but if that's all you have, then use that. The best way to express this is as a timeline: What were the milestones you reached so far? Did you do user testing? Hire staff? Raise money? Incorporate the company? Run minimum viable product (MVP) experiments? List the milestones that you think will facilitate illuminating conversations between you and the investors. Ensure that you're showing off what you've been working on. Use your milestones slide as an opportunity to illustrate how you and your co-founders work together and how you built the earliest, faltering steps of your company.

What are the MVPs?

Another approach to traction is to pre-emptively consider what the most significant assumptions are in your business. Say, for example, that you are developing a smart golf ball that can help players become better golfers. How do you know that people want this? You could spend a fortune developing the product, but the more fundamental question is "does anyone want this?" There are creative ways of testing this, and this is known as an "MVP"—or a minimum viable product. The terminology here is terrible; what you are building is neither a product nor is it viable as a product. Think of an MVP as the smallest amount of resources you can commit to getting the answer to something important about your company.

MVPs can take any shape. They could be a video, a survey, a mock landing page on a website, or a quick product experiment. The goal isn't to build something long-lasting; it's merely an experiment that can help your project fail as quickly as possible. It may sound strange that you want to fail, but trust me, failing fast is the best thing you can do. The worst thing that happens to startups is that they spend years in research and development and end up launching a product that nobody wants or where it turns out that only 20% of the product is useful to your target audience. It would be much better to find out early that what you're building doesn't make sense—that's where MVPs come in.

For example, you could create a website where people can buy these balls and create an advertising campaign driving people to this page—even if you don't yet have the balls in stock. This is all about customer research—so use this opportunity to test price points, messaging, feature sets, or even the colors of the balls. You will find out what your initial customer acquisition cost is, and you can send a survey to your customers. When they make it to the checkout page, you have your answer: yes, somebody was willing to pay for this product. How you design your experiment depends on exactly what question you want answering, but these types of tests can go a long way toward telling the story of why someone should invest in your product. If the top reason that someone won't invest in your startup is that they doubt anybody wants your product, you have now proven otherwise. It may be weird to think of MVP experiments as "traction," but that's what it is. It shows that your founding team can think strategically and critically about how to approach a market. Getting answers to fundamental questions about your business is extremely valuable.

Before you have "real" metrics, you're asking investors to "invest in the dream." There is nothing yet indicating that what you're doing is going to work. In my experience, this is often one of the main reasons that investors turn down early-stage companies. "Come back when you can show some traction" is a ubiquitous rejection note. If you're unable to raise money for your company at this stage, it may be time to take another approach. By any means possible, find a traction metric that you can start building, and focus your attention on moving that metric in the right direction. Tracking metrics will do your fundraising story a world of good. It will help keep your company scrappy and hungry while you're trying to build early versions of your product and find early indicators of product/market fit.

Slide: The Moat

Why is it hard for other startups to do what you're doing?

Of course, you have personal reasons for wanting to start a particular company. Usually, that is because you have a connection to the problem or the market. If your company has a "superpower"—something that makes you extraordinarily well qualified to start the company—consider dedicating some time to telling that part of the story.

Named after the water-filled ditch dug around old castles, in startup land, your natural defense against competitors is known as a "moat." This moat can take many different forms, and not all companies have one—at least not at first. For example, there were at least seven major search engines active on the Internet before Google came along. These days, Google's moat is its sheer market dominance. Commanding an impressive 92% of search traffic in the United States in 2019, it's tough to compete with the search giant, but not impossible. Incumbents are overthrown all the time: at one point, AltaVista had 20% of all search traffic (with Google only taking around 6%), while MySpace dominated the nascent social media market. Both AltaVista and MySpace are mere footnotes in the history of the Internet these days. In 1968, Toyota had about a 0.5% market share in the United States. Today, they are the third best-selling car brand—and they have the #1 best-selling passenger vehicle in the United States, the Toyota Camry. As I am writing this, it seems unlikely that Google, Facebook, Apple, and Netflix will disappear, but, again, not impossible. Consider this: 25 years ago, of those four tech giants, only

© Haje Jan Kamps 2020
H. J. Kamps, *Pitch Perfect*, https://doi.org/10.1007/978-1-4842-6065-4_11

Apple existed, and it was on the brink of bankruptcy as Steve Jobs stepped back in as "interim CEO" in 1997.

Your moat could be many things that are not related to market share, but if you are going to claim to have a moat as part of your slide deck, it has to be real. It will need to be something that makes it genuinely hard for competitors to come and eat your lunch. Your team is probably the first place to look—if you have a team of PhDs who are legitimately the foremost experts in the world on the product you are building, that could form part of your defenses. A weaker case is to have a team that has spent decades in the industry where you're starting the business—it's better than nothing, of course, and in-depth domain knowledge goes a long way. But it isn't exclusive: there are usually many people who have in-depth knowledge about various industries. Seeing your company be successful may bring them out of the woodwork.

Being first to market isn't a guaranteed victory either. There were shovel loads of search engines before Google. There was a smattering of smartphones before the iPhone. There were many music-streaming services before Spotify. If you innovate, know that there will be others with better systems, more developed supply chains, and better-resourced research and development teams than yours. Being first to market means you get to define the market, but it doesn't inoculate you from competitors who get the benefit of learning from your mistakes and missteps.

Other ways of thinking about the moat include a head start on the product; if you're building something genuinely sophisticated, where it would take a long time to replicate the research and development on your product, that could work. As long as your competitors can't buy one of your products, "borrow" all of the innovations, and ship a slightly cheaper or slightly better product quickly.

Patents or other protections can help keep competitors at bay. If the potential number of customers you have is small, you could corner the market by signing your customers to exclusive contracts. Trade secrets are harder to defend, but if you're able to make the case that what you are developing is hard to copy, and a secret worth keeping (as in Figure 11-1), then you're onto something.

Warning When claiming a "moat" as part of your pitch, be very careful. A lot of the time, when I work with clients, the moats they are describing aren't as deep and unpassable as they would claim.

Your customers only care about resolving their challenges or reducing their pain points. They don't particularly care about how the problems are solved. One example of this is Netflix; at one point, they were all in on DVD rentals.

It was a robust and profitable business, and the company could easily have continued to invest in that side of the company right up to the point of bankruptcy. We all know what happened to DVD rentals. Netflix is an example of a company that dared to see the future and adapt accordingly. Crucially, the company knew what problem it was solving for its customers. It wasn't "I want DVDs to turn up in the mail," it was "I want to see great TV and movies, as conveniently as possible." Many companies failed to understand the problem they were solving, and most have been all but forgotten today.

Why us: The moat & the magic

- 20+ years of industry experience

- Trade-secret: Best algorithm for classifying and recommending beer taste profiles

- Independent: Not aligned with any particular brewery or geography

Figure 11-1. Your "moat" is something that makes it hard for other companies to catch up to you. Patents, trade secrets, unusual market dynamics, and deep industry expertise are great examples. Image Source: karandaev/stock.adobe.com

Another excellent example of knowing the problem you are solving is the channel tunnel from the UK to France. The projection was that as soon as the tunnel opens, everything would change. "Faster and more convenient" and "The only way to get to and from the mainland" were the main selling points for the tunnel. But, of course, people had been traveling between the UK and France for thousands of years already—by boat. When the tunnel opened, the ferries responded by refurbishing the fleet and dropping prices to stay competitive. Slower, yes, but cheaper. At the same time, budget airlines continued to do a booming business. All of which is to say, on paper, your solution may seem as obviously the best way to solve a problem, but if your customers disagree, your moat may not be as strong as you think.

Patents are a powerful tool, of course, but they tend to be very specific. Remember that companies build value by resolving a problem for a customer. Your patent will be related to your particular solution, but in the majority of cases, there is more than one way to solve a problem. Put differently, it doesn't help to have a patent on a tunnel under the English Channel if people just take a plane or a boat to accomplish the same thing.

Powerful moats

There are a few truly powerful moats. If you can tap into them, you are onto something good. One is the network effect, which is the idea that every additional person on the network adds value to the whole system. The telephone is a good example here; if you are the only person in the world with a phone, it's useless. The more people have phones, the more valuable it becomes to have a phone yourself. Facebook is tapping into the network effect—if you've ever tried to stop using Facebook, you realize that a lot of events are announced and organized on Facebook. Without a Facebook account, you risk missing an invitation.

The other lock-in mechanism being aware of is the platform effect. eBay is a great example. Of course, you can go to another platform to sell that bread-maker you got as a wedding present, but you know that the largest number of potential buyers are on eBay. The same goes for Uber or Lyft. You may have a preference for Lyft, but if you are in a city where there are ten Uber drivers for every Lyft driver, you have a problem: if you want to go anywhere, you will probably need to use Uber. The other part of the platform effect is that all of these sales are "conquest sales." In other words, you only need one driver to take you from point A to point B. When you choose Uber over Lyft, not only does Uber make money, Lyft effectively loses a potential sale. Platform effects are incredibly powerful, and that's part of the reason why creating platforms is so tricky—and so lucrative, when you get it right.

Network and platform effects are hard to tap into as an early-stage company—per definition, you don't have that many customers yet. However, if your business relies on these market dynamics, it can be powerful to add to your pitch narrative that you have a plan for how to build and leverage them.

Slide: Business Model

How are you going to make money?

Understanding the financial dynamics that underpin your business is a crucial part of being a successful startup founder. When you think "business model," don't fall into the trap of thinking just about the money flowing into the business. In the broadest possible sense, your "business model" is every advantage you have, every asset you can leverage, and everything you do to get customers, serve them well, and generate revenue.

Tip Read *Business Model Generation* by Osterwalder and Pigneur (John Wiley and Sons, 2010) and create a business model canvas (BMC) for your company to understand the full depth of how your business operates. It's usually easiest to create your first BMC as part of a workshop, so see if there's anyone near you facilitating those soon.

At the very least, your business model should comprise of your cost of acquiring customers (CAC) and the amount of money you generate from each customer over their lifetime—or lifetime value (LTV).

© Haje Jan Kamps 2020
H. J. Kamps, *Pitch Perfect*, https://doi.org/10.1007/978-1-4842-6065-4_12

A path to a business model

For a lot of venture-backed companies, optimizing for revenue too early comes at the cost of growth. In other words, if you try to pull out all the stops to generate cash from your customers too soon, you'll probably stunt the customer growth of the company, which is a contraindicator for how well you're doing. I usually advise my clients that they should think about how to get a large number of customers before they worry too much about exactly how much money they are going to make. The main reason for that, from a storytelling point of view, is that you can benchmark revenue-generating companies, and they start to look a lot like growth-stage companies. Counterintuitive as that might be, you don't want to step into growth stage too early.

As much as you don't want to optimize for revenue too soon, you do need to have a clear plan in place for how your company is going to shift gears into generating revenue. That's where your business model will come in.

When it comes to cash, there are a vast number of approaches you can take, and it's a good idea to consider them in some detail. As a consumer, you're used to certain types of transactions already, but don't be fooled into thinking that those are the only options you have available to you.

There's no business without cash

You can sell a product for cash (Casper mattresses is a good example). Subscription models work great (Native deodorants is an example of this in the world of physical products; Netflix is an excellent example of subscription-based entertainment. Stitch Fix is another variant). There are also hybrid models, where you sell a product and attach a subscription. Peloton and its exercise bikes fit into this category. You may also be familiar with advertising models, as exemplified by Facebook, Instagram, and news websites.

Some companies have found great success with "freemium" models—where the basic version of the service is available for free, but that you pay in order to get the full version. For example, Spotify has a free tier that includes adverts. If you don't want the adverts, you can become a subscriber.

Affiliate revenue is another possibility—executed fantastically by the Wirecutter.com website. Wirecutter commissions experts to write best-in-class reviews of certain groups of products, such as best Wi-Fi, best vacuum cleaner, or best slow cooker. The site links to Amazon and other retailers using an "affiliate link." For every item that is sold after you click a link, they get a percentage of the revenue.

Marketplace business models are complicated, but—as I mentioned elsewhere in this book—can be fantastically lucrative. Because you're a middleman, you typically don't have to keep inventory or run warehouses, which makes it much cheaper to operate the business than if you were an online retailer. The downside is that you need to build both the supply side (people selling stuff) and the demand side (people buying stuff) at the same time. eBay and Airbnb are the most prominent examples. In the "sharing economy," there are several other good examples. Postmates is a platform between drivers and restaurants. Uber is a marketplace of sorts, matching cars to passengers who need a ride. Lugg matches van and pickup owners with people needing to move house, and many more.

In the business-to-business realm, there are many other business models in play as well. Licensing is one approach; franchising is another. In the world of solar, you might come across "power purchase agreements"—where the solar power installation company will install solar panels on your home for "free" in exchange for getting some of the solar power generated. In automotive, some car manufacturers are offering all-inclusive rental plans, including insurance, maintenance, and often with free swaps when you get bored of your car.

It's also possible to do partnerships or co-sales. You may develop a piece of technology that is a natural fit for a certain product, for example, and then agree with the manufacturer of that product to bundle your product with theirs. Akrapovič is one example of this—the company makes high-end after-market motorcycle exhaust systems. On some high-end sports motorcycles, you can order the bikes from the manufacturer with an Akrapovič exhaust already fitted. It makes sense for the consumer—it means you don't have to discard a perfectly fine exhaust to upgrade it. It helps the manufacturer generate a bit more cash per motorcycle sold, and it helps the exhaust company create extra sales. A sign of a great business mind is whether you're able to identify how your company can help other companies in a win-win situation.

Whatever business models you end up with, it's crucial that you have a firm grasp of the dynamics in yours—and to show how your company could start generating revenue—as in Figure 12-1.

The summary of business models isn't meant to be an exhaustive list of business models available—there are many more, some more obscure than others. The purpose of this list is to get your creative juices flowing: Can you think of other ways that your company could be generating revenue? What would it look like if that was the only way your startup made money?

Pricing and Business Model

To the customer...

- $400 deposit, refundable after 3 years
- $99 per month subscription
- Includes rental of kegerator
- Includes one keg per month
- Additional kegs at $49

To BeerSub.com...

- $153.90 blended CAC
- Avg subscription is 21 months
- Avg LTV is $2,494.80
- Avg COGS per customer is $1,140
- Avg gross profit per customer: $1,200 over 2 years.

Figure 12-1. I give BeerSub.com a C+ for this slide. It's not uncommon to include a slide for pricing models, if they are particularly complicated, but in this case, the pricing and business models are both relatively straightforward. This slide is at the very upper limit of how much text I'm comfortable with on a slide—I would probably recommend splitting this part of the deck into two different slides or leave the pricing model off the slide altogether. Image Source: breakingthewalls/stock.adobe.com

Weaving the narrative

In your pitch, it's important to be able to tell a solid, coherent narrative of your business plan. Where do customers come from? What does it cost (in terms of effort and cash) to acquire those customers? What would it take to increase your customer base at ten times your current rate? Similarly, how will you be generating revenue from your customers? What are the opportunities to increase your lifetime value per customer?

Having a separate slide for your business model isn't appropriate on all slide decks—but if you're planning on doing something unusual, definitely consider including it. I usually recommend having a business model slide in the appendix, at least; if you don't use it, at least you've made it so you have clarity and can explain how it all comes together. If you do need it, well, flick to the back of your presentation, and there you are!

Slide: Go-to-Market Strategy

What's the "beachhead audience," and how are you going to reach them?

There is a paradox at the heart of building a company. On the one hand, to be VC investable, you need to create a multibillion-dollar company. On the other, you can't start off building every aspect of your company right from day one.

In early-stage companies, even if you know the market pretty well, there's a risk of loss of focus. Every time you turn over a new rock, you'll find seven new opportunities lurking. Inexperienced entrepreneurs won't believe their luck: Look! There is so much gold just lying around in the streets! All we have to do is to pick it all up! The problem, of course, is that each opportunity requires a slightly different approach, and this triggers two potential avenues that don't work. Either you try to build a broad suite of products that serve every opportunity you find. The problem with this is that you're a startup. Per definition, you're woefully under-resourced. Trying to build a whole suite of products is a surefire way to sink your company before it's even up and running. The other approach is to create a "one-size-fits-all" solution. That might work, but the problem is that your target customers are probably

© Haje Jan Kamps 2020
H. J. Kamps, *Pitch Perfect*, https://doi.org/10.1007/978-1-4842-6065-4_13

already using a one-size-fits-all solution to their problem. Convincing them to switch is hard, especially if your solution has a bunch of features that they don't want or need.

Painting a picture of your solution

The solution at the earliest stages of building a company is to take a broad approach in your pitching. You believe you know something about what the world will look like 10 years from now, and how your company can help move the world in that direction. You tell the story of your big-picture vision—this is the story of how you are building a billion-dollar company. Once you've done that, it's time to use the magic phrase. "So that is our big-picture vision for the company. Let me tell you where we are going to start."

In military parlance, the beachhead is where you start your attack. Just taking the beach doesn't help you win the battle—but without a place to begin your assault, you'll never win the war. As much as I hate war metaphors in startup contexts, this one is pretty helpful—building your big, world-changing company is the war. But, just like with any strategy, you have to be conservative with how you deploy your resources.

As a military strategist, putting all your soldiers on the wrong beach is hard to recover from. As a startup strategist, that is what you have to do. Figure out where you're going to start, and then commit 100%. The reason for this is that you are testing ideas. If you believe that your toothpaste startup will do best with mothers-of-two in rural areas, then prove that fully. If you only commit 50% to that strategy, you won't know if it worked or not: Did it fail because your approach is wrong? Or did it fail because you didn't try hard enough? The most awkward meeting you'll ever have with your board is trying to explain why you didn't believe enough in your go-to-market strategy to commit fully.

The hard thing, of course, is that there may be more than one strategy that works—but that's not the point. You only have to find one that you believe in and commit. That is where your beachhead slide comes in—see Figure 13-1. There is no "right" answer to where you focus your go-to-market efforts. Facebook famously started its rollout to an ultraexclusive group of US colleges. The buzz that created, as it rolled out to Ivy League after Ivy League, turned out to be a massive advantage for the small startup. Geographic rollouts can be helpful for physical products; it makes logistics more accessible, and you can potentially dispatch engineers to the location to identify teething problems.

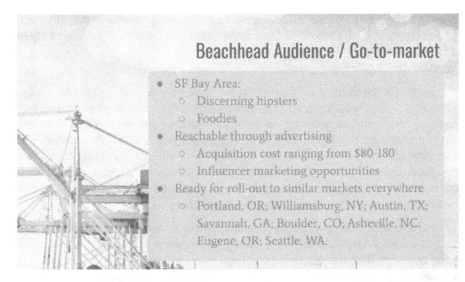

Figure 13-1. Sales and marketing will be a huge part of the operations of your company, and it is often hard to distil a whole marketing strategy into a single slide. Many founders I work with have a separate deck for their sales and marketing efforts, which investors spend more time much later in the due diligence process. For your initial pitch deck, it's helpful to be able to show that you've done your homework and that you have a firm grasp on how you are going to get your first few million dollars worth of revenue. Image Source: artnature/stock.adobe.com

You can slice the market by a near-infinite number of criteria. Consider age, socioeconomic background, geography, interests, marital status, car owner status, media consumption habits, and much more.

Out of all the dozens of opportunities you've identified, where are you placing your chips? Why do you think that this particular market or demographic is particularly representative of your company? What are you hoping to learn from this market, and how will that apply to other markets?

Marketing and segmentation

As I mention, there is no "right" answer, but in the context of a venture capital pitch, there are "wrong" answers. The most significant opportunity to shine on the go-to-market slide is to show that you know how to think through the marketing and sales strategy for your market segment.

On your slide, include information about how many people you expect to reach in this segment. The right number varies wildly based on whether you are a B2B or B2C startup: for business sales, three or four big customers may represent a huge win. For example, if you manufacture memory chips and you land Apple as a client, that could make or break your company. Although come to think of it, if your customer is Apple, it will probably make and break your company. In the world of consumer products, three or four sales may be a failure: if you are Apple, and you only sell three iPhones, that's not going to do your stock price any good.

As part of this slide, you should know how you are going to reach your customers. Are you operating a sales team? Are you buying advertising? Events? Will you be working with influencers to do marketing that way? Would there be billboards alongside the road? Are you doing a direct mail campaign? Do you have an existing email list you will be leveraging? If you have a mixed channel marketing approach, how effective do you expect each channel to be, and how much money are you spending? Finally, you should know how scalable your marketing channels are.

Telling the story of your go-to-market plan is an exercise of applying your tactics to your strategy. In your initial go-to-market activities, the vision for your company first starts gaining traction; these are the steps you are planning to take to get your product into the hands of your customers. It's the first step toward building a robust feedback loop that helps inform your marketing, product, and product/market fit. In a fundraising context, it's good to remind yourself that your investors don't necessarily have to agree with you on what your go-to-market strategy is. For most investors, it's more important that they follow your thought process. They aren't investing in the specific approach you are outlining in your deck—they are investing in the brain that came up with that approach.

Slide: Competitors

Who else is in the market? How else are your customers solving the same problem?

In Chapter 8, we talked about how to determine the size of your market; that's a crucial part of the story. It does miss out on an essential piece of the puzzle: who else is trying to solve this problem? Generally described as your "competitor" slide, this part of the narrative helps confirm that you know the market you are operating in well.

Competitive alternatives

I want to get something important out of the way before we say anything else: some clients I work with say that they don't have competitors. With extremely few exceptions, that is both objectively wrong and the wrong thing to say. If you are entering a market where there are no competitors at all, ask yourself, "Why is nobody solving this problem?" If nobody is generating cash from the problem you are solving, there's a real risk there isn't a market at all.

© Haje Jan Kamps 2020
H. J. Kamps, *Pitch Perfect*, https://doi.org/10.1007/978-1-4842-6065-4_14

An alternative way to think about your competitors is, "What is the problem, exactly, and how are my customers currently solving this problem?" In some cases, there may not be any direct competitors, but there will almost certainly be competitive alternatives. For example, if your company was the first company to build dishwashers, you don't have any direct competitors—yet. But of course, dishes got clean before dishwashers came along. Washing dishes by hand, using disposable utensils and flatware, and employing a maid to clean dishes for you are alternative ways of solving the problem. If you are solving a problem along those lines, saying "we have no competitors" is true— but not helpful for your fundraising narrative.

Competitors

When talking about your competitors, many founders are dismissive or contemptuous about the existing players. I would urge strongly against that. If all goes according to plan, you'll put them out of business soon enough—but until you have the traction and market dominance that is needed to do that, it can't harm to be humble. You may need the incumbents as partners, or they may be potential buyers of your company. Less relevant to pitching, but an interesting point to consider from a company culture point of view, your future customers are likely the customers of an incumbent at the moment. You don't want to start a relationship with a new customer from a position of lack of respect.

Assuming you do have direct competitors, you are doing something a little bit different than incumbents—highlighting the differences is the name of the game here. Perhaps your solution is cheaper, more productive, faster, or addresses the problem differently.

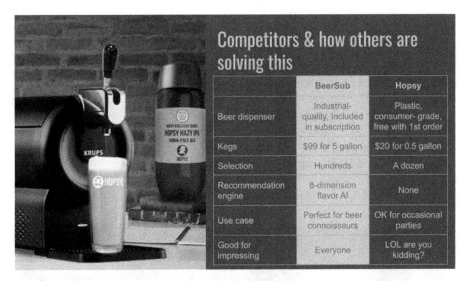

Figure 14-1. The side-by-side grid is a tried-and-tested way to compare competitors. In this case, BeerSub.com is only comparing itself to one competitor—which is likely to cause some discussion as part of the pitch. Showing 3–4 competitors on a grid or 8–10 on a "competitor compass" is probably a more elegant solution. A sample competitor compass can be seen later in this section

Understand your competitors profoundly. How do *they* get customers? How do they serve their customers? Are their customers happy? If you have a small number of very obvious competitors, you could do a lot worse than tracking down some of their customers and run a focus group with them. What do they love, and what do they hate?

Your investors will probably check out your competitors as part of the due diligence process. Having a deeper understanding of the competition than what they can unearth in their due diligence is helpful—and good business hygiene as well.

Don't let your competitors influence you too much. From their products, you can probably deduce the "what," but you cannot presume to know the "why." Your startup is entering the industry because it wants to change how things are done. That's powerful and useful—don't be afraid to carve out your own path.

The vast majority of what you need to know about your competitors will probably not come up in your VC pitch—but that's okay. Like you should have in-depth knowledge about the problem, market, and your solution, having more information than anyone could want about your competitors is crucial.

As far as a slide goes, there are many ways of presenting competitor information to your investors. Do recall, though, that you're not just comparing your product to theirs. You're showing how their company is similar to and different than yours. Some people like showing this as a grid (Figure 14-1), where you can show off your strengths vs. the competitor's. Others like using a two-axis graph (Figure 14-2), usually placing your startup in the top right corner. The axes depend on what the strengths and weaknesses of your company are. The main problem is that it's rarely possible to tell the full story of a competitor landscape on a single slide—but the goal is to put enough collateral on a slide to spark a good conversation. It also helps if you're able to add enough competitors on the slide that the investors have a starting point for their own due diligence research.

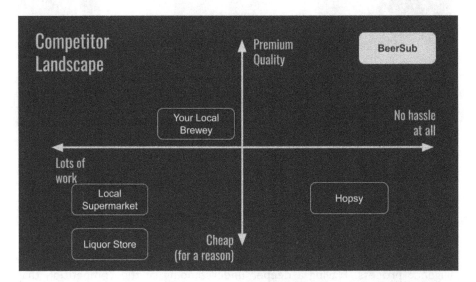

Figure 14-2. Using a "competitor compass" is a quick way to show how you position yourself in the market vs. your competitors. For BeerSub, the axis I chose was hassle vs. quality, but I could just as easily have used quality of recommendations, variety of beers, or any number of other metrics. If you include one of these, make sure that all your major competitors are listed; it's pretty embarrassing to realize you've missed out a big key competitor. Some in-depth Google research right before you go it to pitch is crucial

In the course of pitching your competitive advantage over the incumbents, your investors may know of one or more competitors that aren't listed in your deck. It's helpful to have the selection criteria for what you included on your slide and what you omitted to hand. Whatever you do, don't lie—if the investor mentions a company you've never heard of, say that they slipped through your research, make a note of it, do your research, and consider emailing the investor with some additional context for how that competitor fits into the landscape.

Slide: The Ask

How much are you raising, and what are you going to accomplish with that money?

If there is one slide founders get spectacularly wrong in their decks, it's this one. Sometimes known as the "the ask," others call it the "use of funds" slide—this is where you reveal how much money you are raising and what you're going to accomplish with the money.

Figuring out how much to raise

Many founders will calculate how much money they need to get through 18 months of development and put that on the slide. Some include a pie chart of how much will go to marketing, overheads, research and development, and so on. The problem here is that venture capital is exceptionally goals oriented. Your company surviving for 18 months is a good sign, of course, but doesn't show specific progress.

Some founders omit this slide altogether. Some founders just stick a number on there. Some add something like, "We are raising $2m at a $20m valuation." None of that works; this slide isn't about you or your startup—it is about what the investor is going to get for the money they invest. Or, put differently, if I write your company a $2m check, what is my money going to buy me? I'm not talking about the number of shares or the percentage of the company. I am talking about progress and milestones. What are you going to accomplish with $2m?

© Haje Jan Kamps 2020

H. J. Kamps, *Pitch Perfect*, https://doi.org/10.1007/978-1-4842-6065-4_15

You would be surprised at how many of my clients don't have clarity on how much money they should raise. Often, they think they should be raising a "seed round," take a look at TechCrunch to see how much similar companies raised as a seed round, and then put that number on the deck. Investors will ask, "how did you decide how much money to raise," and poor quality entrepreneurs won't have an answer. The problem is that more often than not, that means they are raising far too much capital—or far too little. Even if the rest of the pitch is excellent, this is an enormous red flag. If the founders don't know how to plan, why should you trust them with money?

You need to know how much money you need to raise. How? Simple: you need to know what you're going to do with the money. Realistically, the amount of money you raise should be enough to get you to the next round of fundraising. That sounds obvious, but how do you know how much that is? That is where your ops plan comes in. In fact, I usually advise my clients to forego an "ask" slide in favor of an operating plan slide instead.

Creating SMART milestones

Your slide needs to answer one question: what milestones do you need to hit to raise the next round of funding?

It's also worth being clear on what your milestones mean. You may have heard of a SMART goal. Your fundraising milestones should be SMART milestones. SMART, in this case, stands for specific, measurable, achievable, relevant, and time based. A poor goal is "Improve marketing," or "Get more customers," or "Add features to our product." An example of a great SMART sales goal might be, "By the end of June 2021, we need 2,000 paying customers on our recurring subscription model." A customer acquisition goal might be, "In the next 6 months, we need to reduce our customer acquisition cost by 20%." A hiring milestone could be, "Our B2B sales need to improve, so by the end of July, we will hire an experienced VP of sales who can help shape our sales processes." Figure 15-1 shows an example "use of funds" slide that has some great SMART goals—and some a poor one. Have a look if you can see which one doesn't work!

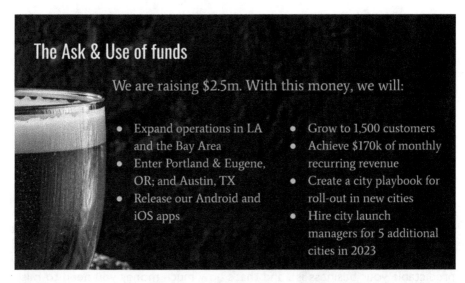

The Ask & Use of funds

We are raising $2.5m. With this money, we will:

- Expand operations in LA and the Bay Area
- Enter Portland & Eugene, OR; and Austin, TX
- Release our Android and iOS apps

- Grow to 1,500 customers
- Achieve $170k of monthly recurring revenue
- Create a city playbook for roll-out in new cities
- Hire city launch managers for 5 additional cities in 2023

Figure 15-1. A clear fundraising goal and well-defined, measurable targets for what will be achieved with the money. Well done, BeerSub.com—this "The Ask & Use of funds" slide is better than 99% of the ones I usually see. I suppose it helps that I created the slide myself. Image Source: tiko_photographer/stock.adobe.com

Once you have clarity on your milestones, you can map them out in a spreadsheet. What resources (time, money, staff) do you need to reach each milestone? Are there dependencies in your plan? Add it all to the sheet. Now, you'll have clarity on what you need to accomplish, how long it will take, and what it will cost.

Bingo. That's the perfect "the ask" slide for your slide deck.

Oh, and remember how I asked you to find the poor "ask" in Figure 15-1? "Expand operations in LA" is bad—because it doesn't define what "expand" means—so it's hard to judge whether or not the goal is completed.

Milestones to consider

For most startups, milestones will include some or all of these things:

- Product – What product milestones do you need to hit in order to raise the next tranche of money? In particular, this includes beta or full product launches, major feature sets in the product pipeline, or integrations with partners.

- Traction – What business metrics do you need to hit to raise more money? How many units do you have to sell? How many subscribers do you need? How many customers do you want? Other metrics may also be helpful here—your net promoter score (NPS), monthly active users, and so on.

- Market validation – What can you do to prove that there's a real market out there willing to pay for the product or service you are peddling?

- Key hires – In order to reach the above goals, you probably need to hire. Who do you need to hire? When?

Map out those milestones, and figure out what resources you need to hit them. That's how much money you need if everything goes to plan. Add 30–70% as a safety buffer (depending on how good your planning is and how predictable your business is), and that's how much money you need to raise. If an investor asks if you have a safety buffer built into your funding round, be honest: they know you'll need it, and good entrepreneurs know that the best laid schemes of mice and men often go awry. You do need to be able to defend the size of the buffer, though – much more than 30% would be an indicator that you don't really know how to plan.

From milestones to a fundraising goal

With all of the above in place, you're in a much better place; you'll be able to see how long it will take to hit the milestones.

Operating Plan					
	H1 2021	H2 2021	H1 2022	H2 2022	2023
# of cities	2	3	5	10	25
BeerSub Staff	4	6	9	20	30
Delivery Staff	4	9	16	35	130
Customers	80	130	1.5k	9k	15k
MRR	$8k	$13k	$170k	$1.1m	$2m
Product Milestones	iOS app in beta	iOS and Android app Live	Rec'n engine live	Affiliate sales engine	Web 2.0 live
Marketing Spend	$15k	$24k	$250k	$1.25m	$2m
Revenue	$35k	$65k	$825k	$5.3m	$19m
Burn	$390k	$650k	$1m	$2.2m	$10m
COGS	$36k	$53k	$575k	$3.3m	$9.5m
Fundraising	$2.5m	-	-	$7.5m	-
EOH Money in Bank	$2m	$1.4m	$400k	$6.3m	$3.6m

Figure 15-2. In addition to "use of money" slide, I recommend having a detailed operating plan slide. Some founders consider the ops plan operationally sensitive and choose to add this to an appendix rather than having it part of the main slide deck—but I really wouldn't start pitching your startup until you have a good high-level operating plan ready. Image Source: Dmitry Lobanov/stock.adobe.com

Don't go into too much detail in your operating plan—you can't predict things that happen 24 months from now, so there's no point in trying. Keep your numbers round and easy to read, and make sure that the next 12–18 months of your operating plan are reasonably detailed. As the founder, that's roughly the amount of time you'll need to hit your milestones and start the fundraising for your next round.

For your pitch deck, you will be able to distill all of the above into a simple table. Use one column per month, and mark out the major milestones and cost centers for your development.

Finally, make sure you do a logic check—in other words, is what you are proposing even possible? If you are going from 10 customers to 10,000 customers over the next 18 months, can the staff you have support the extra customers? Does marketing spend seem reasonable? Does the scale of the operating expenses make sense along with the number of customers? If all of those things look right, then you're probably on your way to having a solid operating plan.

One final thing, if you don't have a term sheet in hand, don't include a valuation on the slide; that's all up for negotiation anyway.

Slide: Timing

Why is now the perfect time to start this company?

All great new companies have something in common; they were the right company, solving the right problem at the right time. For every colossal startup success, you'll often hear, "Oh! That thing? Jenny was working on that like a decade ago." Jenny—whoever she is—is now working on a new startup, because she failed to find traction and product/market fit for her thing.

I usually advise against a "timing" or "why now?" slide in a pitch deck. I considered not including this chapter in the book. However, the "why now" slide just won't die—and for some companies, putting their vision into a historical context is crucial.

Skate to where the puck is going

Timing is a delicate matter because while it's often possible to see some significant market trends converging, the question of timing is one of reading the future. In the words of Wayne Gretzky, you want to be skating to where the puck will be, not where the puck is. In other words, if you're going to build an incredible cryptocurrency startup, you usually don't want to be the founder that started a company the day Bitcoin hit $20,000. (As I'm writing this, BTC has been hovering at around $10k for the best part of a year). The perfect founder was already deep in the crypto world, had faith in cryptocurrencies

© Haje Jan Kamps 2020
H. J. Kamps, *Pitch Perfect*, https://doi.org/10.1007/978-1-4842-6065-4_16

in general, and was already building a company long before Bitcoin rallied. If you were building a crypto startup in 2010—before any of the cryptocurrencies were making it big—you probably would need to explain why you think now is the time to start your company.

Let me bring this to life with an example: when consumer-grade photography drones first started happening, the "why now" question was necessary. Yes, it's refreshing to have a flying camera and all, but why did they arrive when they did? After all, RC planes and helicopters have been around since the 1970s. Compact video cameras (such as GoPros) have been around for a good while, too. It would have been possible to build a quadcopter for a long time (the first helicopter was a quadcopter, back in 1920), but it would have been an academic experiment. In essence, the technology required would have been prohibitively expensive for a consumer-grade piece of tech. What unlocked photography drones? The prevalence of Apple's iPhone did.

As smartphones became ubiquitous, small camera modules, solid-state accelerometers, radio, and GPS chipsets all became dirt cheap and hackable. If you are pitching one of the first consumer-grade quadcopter startups, you had better include a "why now" narrative. In the case of quadcopters, you could even extend the story by saying that all the technology is now available, and there will inevitably be at least some market for these products.

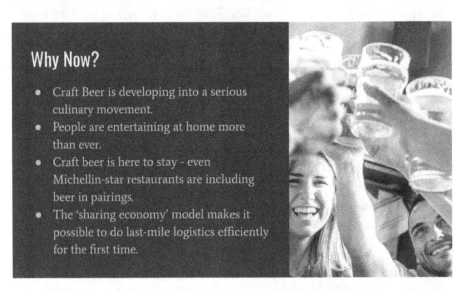

Why Now?

- Craft Beer is developing into a serious culinary movement.
- People are entertaining at home more than ever.
- Craft beer is here to stay - even Michellin-star restaurants are including beer in pairings.
- The 'sharing economy' model makes it possible to do last-mile logistics efficiently for the first time.

Figure 16-1. One of my favorite questions to ask founders is "why couldn't you have done this 5 years ago?" and "why is 5 years from now too late?" The very best companies are started because they have seen something change in the market, in the availability of technology, or a scientific breakthrough. What are the keys that unlock the startup? Your "why now" slide tells that story. Image Source: Mirko/stock.adobe.com

Why now?

"Why now" can be the question that unlocks a lot of different conversations. If you are Slack or Zoom, you can use the trend toward remote working to tell the story of your company being in the right place at the right time. If you are an Internet-of-things company, it's an excuse to talk about the technological developments that have come before you. Any big-picture behavior change or market shifts can be woven into your narratives to help bolster your story—as shown in Figure 16-1.

The most successful startups of our era did three things: They spotted a trend early and developed a solution to take advantage of that. They rode the wave as the entire market grew; effectively, they were expanding both by increasing market share and through the fact that the whole market was developing. Slightly later in their journey, they became the poster child for that market, helping it grow further. Google, Facebook, and Apple are all good examples here; they aren't the first search engine, social network, or smartphone/computer manufacturer. What did these companies get right? They saw an opportunity: a universe where people needed better versions of all of these products. They were able to build solutions that were better than anything else out there. Then they ended up defining the industries they entered, riding the wave to the top.

Uber is another excellent example; they started as a taxi service with an app to call a cab. Before smartphones, Uber wouldn't have been possible. When more and more people began carrying devices with GPS and data network capabilities, a new opportunity was unlocked. Instead of having to call a taxi firm, you could press a button. Uber's original innovation was replacing the dispatcher. Then something happened: Airbnb was starting to take off, and people started wondering what else could be part of the sharing economy. Lyft invented modern ride sharing as we know it today, and Uber took a look over its shoulder and figured they could execute better. And they did, quickly gobbling up a significant market share. But what happened to Lyft? They were left in the dust by Uber, but the company still managed to proliferate by becoming a challenger brand with a better reputation than the market leader. As I'm writing this, Uber's market cap (i.e., the value of the company) is five times bigger than Lyft's—but Lyft itself is worth $11bn, which is nothing to scoff at.

Reiterate your strengths

In my experience, you can use your timing narrative to reiterate some of the biggest strengths in your startup. You should explain the macro-dynamics of your space. Please explain how the market is evolving and how new technological innovations make your company possible when it wasn't before.

Remind the investors how changes in regulatory frameworks are opening new opportunities: demographic shifts (the population as a whole is aging), technology shifts (self-driving cars, solar power, electric vehicles, 5G mobile phone networks), market shifts (homeownership numbers, market boom/bust times), and significant changes in how work is done (the gig economy, working from home, remote-first companies). Many of these trends are somewhat predictable. The best startup founders know how to spot them and leverage them to their advantage.

It's an opportunity to remind investors how your team has been in this industry for a long time. "I saw all of these shifts happen when I was a VP of investment banking at Goldman Sachs for 15 years" is a great way to remind the investors that you have both experience and in-depth domain knowledge.

The critical point here is that the "why now" is partially about history, but remember that it's not a history lesson—it is about trends. You can use past data and innovation to draw a trend line toward the future. Combine that with what your company is doing and where it is going. The perfect "why now" slide has a fast-moving puck and a startup moving at breakneck speed to intercept it where it's going to be in 5 years. It's going to be a hell of a challenge, but this is the sort of thing that makes investors salivate; the world's most significant opportunities are high-risk, high-reward movements. Think big, and weave a story of how you are on the right vector to be in the right place at the right time.

The Take-Home Deck

Should you have multiple versions of your pitch deck? Maybe…

You don't necessarily even *need* a deck to deliver a great pitch. I co-founded my company LifeFolder with Colin Liotta. The company made a conversational interface ("chatbot") company that was all about guiding people through their first conversation about death. At the beginning of a pitch, I'd ask the investors, "I have a pitch deck, but we're about to spend an hour talking about death. Do you want to see the deck, or would you like to have a conversation?" Of course, that opening gambit was part of the pitch. With one exception, investors chose the conversation. That was precisely the point of the startup; that conversations are the best tool for the emotionally intense subject matter at hand.

Sleight of hands where you are doing Jedi mind tricks aside, you're probably going to need a pitch deck—even if you're not using it in your pitch, it's useful as a mental model to help you keep track of where you are in your story.

© Haje Jan Kamps 2020
H. J. Kamps, *Pitch Perfect*, https://doi.org/10.1007/978-1-4842-6065-4_17

How many decks do you need?

A question that comes up with some regularity is how many decks you need. As we discussed in Chapter 3, your presentation deck should have as little text on it as you can get away with. That works when you are presenting, and you use the slides as prompts for yourself, to show photos or graphs, or if you want to emphasize the key points you are making for your investors. That isn't the only way a deck is used. You will also hear about a "send-ahead deck" or a "leave-behind deck."

To figure out how to customize the decks, think about how your recipients will use them. The send-ahead deck is for an investor to decide whether to take a meeting. They may also use it to prepare ahead of a phone screen. The leave-behind deck is for an investor to revisit your pitch and to look more closely at the details (especially financial tables or graphs) after you've left the meeting.

Some founders decide to make one deck, but as with all one-size-fits-all solutions, there are challenges with this. There will be a temptation to include more information than you strictly need on the presentation deck, so it makes sense without a voice-over. This can result in a messy deck stuffed with too much information. On the other hand, if you try to send a deck that only has graphs and photos on it, it is hard to make sense of it in isolation, without additional context.

My approach is to spend 80% of your time on the presentation deck. Ultimately, this is where the rubber hits the road; convincing someone to invest will happen in your pitch meetings and the conversations with your investors. In the process of creating your pitch, you are creating your narrative of your startup. Once you have a pitch and a deck you are happy with, think about what other collateral you need to complete the process.

Alternative decks

For the send-ahead deck, I've seen founders create a one-pager that summarizes the main reasons why the company will be successful. The one-pager is usually a PDF summarizing the entire pitch on a single page, with some graphics or charts to underline the salient points. Another approach is to create a "teaser deck"—instead of including all the points that are relevant to the pitching process, you add the three to four showstopper slides. If your team is world class, include a team slide. If your traction is taking off, lead with your traction slide.

The other common approach is to create a separate deck for emailing. You present from your great-looking presentation deck, but if someone wants to see the deck in advance or after your pitch, you send the investors a version that works on its own. With this approach, you should use the same order and headlines for each slide, but add more text to help make the narrative, so the slides tell the full story of what you are trying to do.

A couple of the startups I've worked with took yet another tack. Instead of spending effort on creating a second design of the deck to make more space for text, they used the "presenter notes" feature in Keynote or PowerPoint to add the additional information, context, and links to external resources. Most presentation software has a feature that enables you to print the slides with your presenter notes alongside it. Use that feature to create PDFs of your slides. Make sure that your slides are still readable at the size they appear on the PDF, but if you followed the "fewer words, larger text" approach to deck design we discussed in Chapter 3, that should work well.

Should you send a deck in advance?

Some founders are worried that if they send a deck to an investor, the investor will leak the deck or share it with one of your competitors. In my experience, that is exceedingly rare, for two reasons. For one thing, your presentation will have confidential information on it, but the magic in company building is in the execution. Even if a competitor had a PDF of your pitch, it wouldn't be all that useful to them. Far more importantly, investors live and die by their deal flow. If they get caught sharing decks, founders will hesitate to reach out to them, which completely ruins the VC business model. Reputationally, VCs have much more to lose on sharing your deck than the tiny incremental improvement they may see in a portfolio company as the result of them having seen your investor story.

You don't need to ask for an NDA before you send a deck—the VCs won't sign it. There is one exception; if you have plans to file a patent, but you haven't filed it yet, and if you are planning to talk about your intellectual property, make sure there is an NDA in place. The worst-case scenario here is that talking about the technology before you file your patent could invalidate the patent. In any case, information that sensitive shouldn't go on a deck, and to protect the defensibility of your patents, you should insist on an NDA being signed before you discuss the details of unfiled patents. If you don't have an NDA in place, don't go into the details. Better yet, get your provisional filing in with the patent office to avoid the problem altogether.

It is safe to send your deck to VCs. If they ask for it, don't push back and don't refuse, but nothing says that you have to send the same version of your presentation deck to them—get creative, and remember that it's all about information exchange. You may be asked for a deck, but usually, the request is actually for a particular set of information. How you convey that information is up to you—send your presentation PDF if you want, or create a separate version of it if you think that tells the story better.

Who Should You Be Talking To?

Creating an investor lead list

Your deck is perfect. Your pitch is tighter than a camel squeezing through the eye of a needle. You've done some stretching, you've had three cups of coffee, and you have even tried your vocal cords at a primal scream in the forest. In short, you're ready to start pitching your startup to investors. How do you find them? That is where a lead list comes in.

A lead list, you'll be unsurprised to learn, is a list of leads for potential investors. To be more specific, it should be a spreadsheet of some sort. Excel works. Google Sheets is better for collaboration. Airtable is excellent if you want to be able to do advanced filtering. You can also decide to use a customer relationship management (CRM) tool. You would typically use a CRM tool for sales processes—which is perfect. When you think about it, your fundraising journey is very much a sales process.

© Haje Jan Kamps 2020

H. J. Kamps, *Pitch Perfect*, https://doi.org/10.1007/978-1-4842-6065-4_18

Structuring the list

Before we talk about how to find your investors, let's take a look at what information you need about each investor:

- The name of the firm
- A link to the firm's website
- The name of the partner at the firm you want to target (if you know)
- An email address for the partner (if you have it)
- Connection vector (i.e., who do you know who can get you an introduction? We will get back to this in the next chapter.)
- Whether the firm leads investment rounds or not
- The size of the fund
- The fund's typical check size
- Relevant investments the firm has made
- Notes and info
- What tier firm it is (I'll talk more about that in just a moment)
- When did the firm start investing out of its current fund

Some of the columns of your spreadsheet are going to be clear. Let's talk about the ones that aren't.

Partners

Different partners at different funds will have varying interests and focus areas. One partner may have an in-depth focus on hardware. Another may be excited about marketplaces. A third might have a soft spot in their heart for healthcare startups. Even if you've seen the firm invest in a bunch of hardware companies, it reflects poorly on you if you end up pitching your healthcare company to the hardware partner. If you know the hardware partner personally, it's possible to send them an email and ask for an intro to the healthcare partner, of course. If you don't have a warm intro, ultimately, the firm will want the deal flow, so if you send your healthcare startup to Henrietta Hardware, she will forward it to Harry Healthcare. Approaching the right person does show that you've done your research, though, so try to get it right; it helps you, it helps them. It's worth noting that not all firms have clear delineations between partners—perhaps the whole firm is focused, or all partners are generalists. In that case, you pitch to the partner you can get the warmest introduction to—we will talk more about warm introductions in the next chapter.

Firms who lead

You should find out whether the firm is willing to "lead" a round or not. Leading an investment means negotiating with you for the terms of the round, doing in-depth due diligence, and writing you the first check for your round. Firms that don't lead will "follow"—they tend to do lighter due diligence, and they accept the same terms as the lead investor. Note that a "follow" investor doesn't necessarily write smaller checks—I've seen examples of a "follow" investor writing checks the same size or larger than the lead investor. You'll also sometimes find that some firms want to co-lead—that is, both dictate terms. I'm less of a fan of that—if I find myself in that situation, I'd try to play it so that I get two term sheets from them. They'll probably be pretty similar, but at least you have two conversations going in parallel. At the beginning of your fundraising process, ignore any firms that don't lead rounds—they are a distraction until you have a term sheet.

Relevant investments

In your research, look for "relevant" investments that the firm has made. Relevant, in this case, doesn't mean direct competitors. It's extremely rare (but not unheard of!) that a firm would invest in two startups that are going head to head. You will be looking for investments in the same space. For example, if your startup is tackling a specific type of cancer, look for firms that have invested in solutions focusing on other types. If you are solving one supply-chain problem with a SaaS solution, look for investors who've placed a bet on SaaS solutions in other parts of the supply chain. When you talk to the investors, mentioning their related investments as part of your pitch is powerful—and if you know the founding teams of the other investments, all the better.

Fund dynamics

The fund dynamics for each firm are essential. You need to know the size of the current fund they are investing out of, the typical check size they write, and when they started investing out of their current fund. The most important of these is the check size. If you are raising $15m, and the fund you have your eyes on only writes $20m checks, that's not a good thing; you aren't a "good deal" for them. In any individual round, a lead investor will typically invest half the money raised. If you are raising $15m, it means that you're looking for a fund that can write a $7.5m check to lead the round. A fund that typically leads rounds and invests $20m per investment is investing in $40m rounds, meaning that you're barking up the wrong tree. Doing your research here is essential. Knowing the size of the fund and when they started investing is helpful, but exactly why is a little outside the scope of this book; make sure you have a good advisor who can talk you through those dynamics and why those two numbers are important to you. Incidentally, asking a potential fundraising advisor to explain what you should be looking for in terms of fund size and fund age is an efficient filter to see whether your advisor is a good fit. If they don't know, or if they can't explain it, run for the hills.

Tier

You should also make a note of what "tier" you think the firm is. A tier is a subjective judgment of how prestigious you believe the firm is. If you get a lead investment from a top-tier firm, it becomes much easier to get other investors interested. If your lead is a low-tier fund, it becomes much harder. More respected firms also make it easier to raise follow-on funding; lower-tier investors tend to want the halo reputation of investing alongside top-tier firms. Note that the "tiers" are often dependent on the industry. In niche industries, a relatively obscure firm (i.e., one that isn't well-known in the broader investor community) can be in high regard among investors investing in that niche. Do your research thoroughly.

Notes

In the notes field, capture rumors and other data points you pick up. If someone tells you that Elena, at a particular firm, has shifted her attention to something relevant to your company, make a note! The VC industry can change quickly, and even though Elena may not have made any investments in your space yet, you could be the first. The only way to find that out is to pay attention and do a lot of networking. Accept coffee invites from anyone who will take a meeting even if they don't plan to invest. If they are willing to share inside gossip about the investment landscape in your industry, that is perfect!

Doing the research

Doing in-depth research to find out who you should reach out to is not trivial. There are more than 700 venture firms in Silicon Valley alone. It's possible that 50 or more would be a good fit for your startup—so how do you find them?

For your first sift of potential investors, I recommend taking a pretty broad approach. The goal is to have a comprehensive long list of all of your potential investors and then prioritize them in the order that makes the most sense for your company.

A technique I've found that will work well is to make a list of 30–40 companies that are slightly more advanced in their journey than you are. If you are raising a seed round, look at companies that are at their series A. This ensures that there's as much data available as possible about their previous fundraising, but also that the data you are gathering is less than 2 years old. For this list of companies, get creative—think of companies that are similar to yours, but not the same. If you are creating a new type of toothbrush, think about tooth-whitening startups. If your product helps learn a new language, list companies that are for other educational sectors. Does your company create a tool that helps reduce the risk of credit cards? List companies that offer other auxiliary services for the credit card industry—rewards programs, marketing tools for credit cards, or credit monitoring applications.

The next step of the research is to use whatever data you can find to learn more about the fundraising journey for these companies. Find out who invested, when, and how much. Databases like PitchBook and Crunchbase are fantastically helpful here—when I work with customers, I tend to use both to help comb the landscape for potential investors. Also, use Google News; do a search for "[company name] funding round" and read whatever press releases or news stories you can find. Make a note of all named investors—and in particular who led the rounds.

The goal of this research is to get a picture of which firms are emerging. Whenever I run this type of research for my own companies or my clients, I am always amazed to see how many times the same firms come up again and again. To me, that's a sign that the technique is working. If I came up with a list of 40 companies that are "relevant" to the startup I'm researching for, and the same 2–3 investors come up again and again, those will pop to the top of my list; clearly, they have a particular interest in this industry or market.

At the end of this research, you should ideally have a list of 50–80 venture firms. Start filtering them down—this is where Airtable comes in handy. Move everyone who doesn't lead rounds to the bottom of the list. Sort everyone else by tier and by how well connected you are to the firms. In a perfect world, three to four firms bubble to the top; they lead investments at the stage where you are raising money. They are prestigious firms. And you have a way of getting a warm connection.

Now that you have your lead list ready to go, it's time to start outreach—more about that in the next chapter!

Getting Introductions

So, how *do* you get in front of the right people?

If you've read anything about pitching your company, you've probably come across advice that says that you need a warm introduction to an investor. Without a doubt, a good, friendly introduction—ideally from a founder they've already invested in—is the best way to get on the radar of an investor. If you don't regularly attend barbecues at the Palo Alto, California, mansions of venture capitalists, don't worry—access isn't the only way to raise money.

As soon as you have your story straight and your deck in order, it's time to get in front of the investors. Here's a few starting points.

Warm introductions

A "warm introduction" is an introduction made by someone the VC knows well, by someone relevant. The VC might know their kids' school teacher pretty well, for example, but the school teacher may not have a lot of startup or investing experience. That's a less warm introduction than one made by a

© Haje Jan Kamps 2020
H. J. Kamps, *Pitch Perfect*, https://doi.org/10.1007/978-1-4842-6065-4_19

founder where the investor has a current investment. Better than that, even, is an introduction from a founder that has already made the investor a lot of money through a previous exit. I don't have to explain how this works; if you know investors personally, schedule a coffee and pick their brains. You don't need an intro for that. If you know other successful startup founders, talk to them; they will make intros if they believe in your vision.

Unless you've been circulating in the startup ecosystem for a long time, the chances are that your list of founder buddies or investor friends is pretty short. Now, you may have to do a bit more work.

The idea of introductions is all about network: it works as a filtering system. Any given founder will forward perhaps one to two deals per month to investors; those go to the top of the list, especially if the introduction adds some context about the strength of the connection. "I've worked with them for 15 years across three companies, and I have invested my own money in this company at the angel stage" is better than "I met them at a party once."

The problem, of course, is that networks can be opaque. Perhaps an old friend you used to work with at Google is a childhood friend of a well-known venture capitalist? Maybe your former boss went on to start a company, raised money from someone relevant to your company, and would love to do an intro?

Mine your LinkedIn connections

LinkedIn is the perfect tool for doing this type of research. In the previous chapter, we made a long list of investors we might want to talk to. Now it's time to continue the research on LinkedIn.

For investment firm you want to talk to, look up your ideal partner on LinkedIn. Check out who your second-degree connections are and email them one by one. Tell them briefly what you are working on and ask them: "How strong is your connection with X? Do you know any other relevant investors in this space?" That does two things: If it's a strong connection, you're ready to ask for an introduction. If it's a weaker connection, keep looking to see if you have a more dependable way in. And, of course, if they know another investor that hasn't come up in your research, that's even better!

If you don't have second-degree connections to a particular partner, widen your search to the other partners and investment professionals in the same firm.

Work your way through the whole list that way. Yes, this is going to take a tremendous amount of time—but it's worth every second.

If you are relatively well connected to the startup ecosystem, you will probably find several connections this way. Ask for introductions from your friends, co-workers, and others who are well connected. It's okay to send through a summary (two to three sentences is excellent), so you can be sure there are no misunderstandings. In the summary, include your elevator pitch. What are you building? What is unique about your startup? How much are you raising?

Once you are connected, the investor will probably ask you to share your deck. At that point, you can expect a quick rejection, for example, if there's no fit between the investor's investment thesis and your startup. I'm covering investment theses—and why you should care—more in the next chapter. If you don't get rejected immediately, the next step is usually a phone screen or a pitch meeting in person. If the introduction is good enough, and the investor has a lot of faith in the person doing the introduction, they will often skip the phone screen and go straight into a pitch meeting.

But what if you can't find that many warm introductions?

Cold emailing

As I mentioned, warm intros are by far the best—but they aren't always possible. If you have enough time, the best approach would be to start networking. Become acquainted with the founders at the startups you found in your research, and see if you can get to know them a bit. Asking for advice sometimes works. Offering help might work. Meeting at networking events can be an excellent way to build your network and get introductions, too.

The truth is, though, sometimes you want to talk to an investor where you don't have an obvious path to their office. If that happens, reaching out cold is the only way. Many people will tell you not to, and it doesn't always work. You have one dynamic in your favor, however. Investors need deal flow; they need to evaluate deals, and they need to make investments. Deal flow can come from almost anywhere—and sometimes through the weirdest of channels. Nearly every investor I know has, at some point, made an investment that started with a cold inbound email, a tweet, or a chance meeting at a networking event.

If you do have to send a cold email, do so with great care and attention. All investors get dozens of cold pitches per day. High-profile investors get hundreds. And the very top investors see thousands. Copying and pasting the same introduction to all your emails isn't going to cut it. Think about it this way: You are sending a cold email that, if everything goes to plan, could get your startup hundreds of thousands, if not millions, of dollars to continue your journey. You can afford to spend some time to add some love, care, and customization to your emails—and investors can spot a copy-and-paste email from a mile away.

A great cold email starts with context: why are you emailing them? Start by adding the custom content: why do you think they are a great investor? "Hi, I am emailing you because I noticed you invested in A, B, and C, and I noticed that you mentioned your hobby X on Twitter. I am building something a little bit similar to those companies—and I love X, too!" That's all it takes. You'll stand out a mile just by that tiny bit of extra research and customization. Now that you have their attention, the next two to three paragraphs sell the highlights of what your company does and why it makes an excellent investment. If you have traction, team, and market, work all three into the initial pitch, but keep the email short—150–200 words at the absolute maximum. Finish the email with a question—and make sure there's only one question in the whole email. "I believe my company would be a great fit with Firm X's investment thesis—would you like to take a closer look at the deck?" is perfect. If they aren't interested, they can ignore it. If they are, all they have to do is reply, "Sure, I'll take a closer look," and you have a conversation going. Make it as easy as possible to open a dialog.

If you don't get a response, think about a way that you can do a follow-up. Reply to your email a week later, ideally, with an additional piece of information. "Just wanted to make sure you saw the below—and I wanted to add, we have just signed a major contract with Microsoft. I would love to tell you more" is perfect. Adding information is a legitimate reason to reach out again. If the additional information adds value to the pitch, they will probably reread your original pitch, and you will almost certainly get a reply if the firm is interested.

The Investment Thesis

Your potential investors have a thesis they use to guide their investments. It's helpful to know what it is

One of the most commonly recurring frustrations I hear from the startups I work with is that rejections from venture capitalists are often extremely vague. There are several reasons why you may get a wishy-washy rejection. A lot of the time, it's because you're talking to the wrong investors.

What makes a "wrong" investor?

Every investment fund has a "thesis" or a set of guidelines that inform how they deploy their investments. If your startup doesn't fit this thesis, chances are it doesn't matter how promising your company is—the investors may hear you out, but they are not going to deploy cash.

© Haje Jan Kamps 2020
H. J. Kamps, *Pitch Perfect*, https://doi.org/10.1007/978-1-4842-6065-4_20

For some funds, this thesis might be extensive ("All early-stage companies in California"), and some can get pretty narrow ("$1m checks into crypto startups founded by Ramapo College graduates with blue hair").

If you fall outside of the "thesis," some investors might still invest—if an auspicious opportunity comes along, they will at least consider it—but remember that the "thesis" is what the investment partners used to raise money from their limited partners (LPs). If a fund starts deploying a bunch of cash into startups that are out of scope compared to the thesis, the LPs will start getting twitchy and lose faith pretty quickly.

What goes into a thesis?

Investment theses will include some combination of the following. Some funds care a lot about some of these things, and some are less sensitive. To some, these things may be a deal-breaker—and others take a more flexible approach.

- **Investment amount** – Most funds have a minimum and maximum check size and a min/max round size.

- **Target audience** – Some funds focus on business-to-business (B2B) companies, where the core sales dynamic tends to be a small number of large sales. Others focus on business-to-consumer (B2C) companies (typically making a large number of smaller sales). Others again invest in B2B2C—companies that supply businesses that supply consumers.

- **Verticals** – Some funds only invest in verticals, while others may explicitly say they avoid specific verticals. Example verticals might be medical tech, education tech, "deep tech," space, crypto companies, surveillance companies, advertising technology, and many more.

- **Ownership targets** – Some funds will only invest if they can own a certain percentage of the company they invest in at the end of the investment round.

- **Education** – Some funds specifically support graduates from a particular school or alumni network. These tend to raise money from the alumni network, too.

- **Demographic** – Some firms focus on investing along demographic boundaries—young founders, older founders, Latinx founders, female founders, founders who have been in prison, and many more.

- **Geographic location** – Almost all investment firms have geographic boundaries for where they source deals. They may invest only within—or without—certain areas, states, countries, or regions.

- **Opportunity size** – Most investors invest in companies that have at least the possibility of an outsize return. In venture capital, most funds try to make investments where there is at least a possibility that every investment "returns the fund." In other words, if they have a $100m fund, and they make $5m investments, they can make 20 investments in total. Each of these investments should have at least the outsize possibility of a 20x return—turning the $5m investment into a $100m return on investment. If your investment is looking interesting, but the investors believe that you would be a 3x return at best, you probably wouldn't raise money.

So, is that all? Well, not quite. All of the preceding points are specifically tied to the thesis of the investor. If you tick all of those boxes, that isn't the end of your journey—that's the beginning. The rest of your pitch still has to be good!

How do you know if your company is a good fit with the thesis?

Ask them. Most investors are happy to tell you what their thesis is.

Ask the question, "What do you typically like to invest in?" and "Do you think my company is a good fit with your thesis?" If you get a "no," it's okay to ask what aspect of your company isn't a good fit. It's possible that they may have misunderstood something and that it's possible to correct the misunderstanding at this point. You wouldn't be the first startup to have been turned down over a misunderstanding.

Further Reading

... Because it's cheaper learning from someone else's mistakes, than it is to make your own

There's a common saying that you should learn from your own mistakes. That is true—but in the world of startups, learning from someone else's mistakes is much faster and cheaper. One way to do that is to read.

Why bother with books in the first place? I would probably counter that with another question—if you cannot commit to reading a few hundred pages about what you're about to embark on, perhaps building your own business isn't for you.

To close out this book, I'd like to share some of my favorites with you. They've all made a big difference in how I think about various aspects of building companies, and they've been hugely inspirational. Enjoy!

The Lean Startup by Eric Reiss is probably going to be your bible. Read it first, and then reread it last. It talks in great detail about how to get to the "nugget" of what you need to learn, and how to iterate quickly to get to a product-market fit.

More venture-funding specific, *Venture Deals: Be Smarter Than Your Lawyer and Venture Capitalist* by Brad Feld and Jason Mendelson is a fantastic resource. It takes you through the whole process, step by step, and in particular, it is helpful to understand all the terminology and the negotiation portion of your fundraising.

© Haje Jan Kamps 2020
H. J. Kamps, *Pitch Perfect*, https://doi.org/10.1007/978-1-4842-6065-4_21

The Mom Test by Rob Fitzpatrick is a beautiful compendium to lean thinking. The basic concept is this: the worst possible person to ask for feedback is your mother. Why? Because the mom archetype is going to want to tell you what you want to hear to support you. This book explains who to ask and what questions to ask to validate your business.

Running Lean: Iterate from Plan A to a Plan That Works by Ash Maurya is a great follow-up from *The Lean Startup*, once your business is up and running. It helps transition from the early-start ideas and ensure that you stay lean as the company develops further.

Despite a similar name to the previous book, *Getting to Plan B* by John Mullins and Randy Komisar is quite a different book; don't ignore one because you've read the other. *Getting to Plan B* is a great exploration into business metrics. How can you tell whether you're doing well, and how can you ensure you continue to improve and innovate?

How to Make Friends and Influence People by Dale Carnegie is one of those books that are not necessarily startup specific, but it's a must-read. It is chocker block with advice that couldn't be more relevant to a startup founder, even though Carnegie wrote it a rather long time ago.

Rework by Jason Fried (of 37 signals/Basecamp fame) is a great short book talking about different ways of launching a software company while staying as lean as possible.

The Thank You Economy by Gary Vaynerchuk is an excellent primer on how to "think different" in the way you interact with, and listen to, your customers. While you are at it, pick up his *Jab, Jab, Jab, Right Hook* as well—it's a fantastic introduction to multimodal marketing in the Internet age.

Delivering Happiness by Tony Hsieh is a fabulous introduction to "customer-focused customer service," which—believe it or not—is remarkably rare. Hsieh is the boss at Zappo's, and they built a whole business on doing customer service preposterously well.

The Tipping Point by Malcolm Gladwell is one of the rare breeds marketing books that is remarkably readable, while also exploring an enormous topic, in this case, what makes something go "viral." A very pleasant read indeed.

The Design of Everyday Things by Don Norman is a classic in the design space—and for a good reason. It makes an eloquent argument for how nothing is ever the user's fault—if you can't figure out how to open a door (is it push or pull?) or how to use your kitchen burners (which one turns on the rear right burner?), that's not your fault—it's a design flaw. The thought patterns discussed in the book are crucial for product designers.

Crossing the Chasm by Geoffry Moore covers a fascinating topic; how do you go from selling to a very interested group of close followers and fans to taking your product mainstream without "selling out"? An incredibly insightful book, but it's probably safe to leave this one until your business is up and running.

Permission Marketing by Seth Godin explores the concept of making your potential consumers interested in what you have to say before you say it. It may be harder to implement in practice than it sounds, but it pays incredible dividends.

Poorly Made in China by Paul Midler is a good read if you're thinking of doing any manufacturing. It's bloody scary, but it does help you place you in the right frame of mind to make some careful decisions.

Everything is Negotiable by Gavin Kennedy was one of those books that completely changed how I saw life—beyond just business. The title does cover the key part of the book, but understanding how to negotiate, what you are negotiating for, and why to negotiate is a crucial life skill.

I

Index

A

Acquisition or initial public offering (IPO), 12

Airbnb, 32, 59

Akrapovič, 59

Amazon Web Services (AWS), 30

Apple, 32

"the ask,"
- market validation, 72
- money, 69, 70
- product, 71
- traction, 72
- use of funds, 70
- use of money, 72, 73

Assets under management (AUM), 10, 12

B

Bill of materials (BOM), 23

Business model
- BMC, 57
- coherent narrative, 60
- freemium models, 58
- growth-stage companies, 58
- high-end sports motorcycles, 59
- hybrid models, 58
- licensing, 59
- marketplace, 59
- money flowing, 57
- power purchase agreements, 59
- venture-backed companies, 58

Business model canvas (BMC), 57

Business-to-consumer (B2C), 3

C

Cold emailing, 91, 92

Competitors
- customers, 67
- pitching, 66
- problem, 66
- VC pitch, 67
- vs. strengths, 68

Cost of acquiring customers (CAC), 48, 57

Cost of goods sold (COGS), 23

Credit card fraud, 22

Customer-focused customer service, 98

Customer relationship management (CRM), 29, 83

D

Direct-to-consumer (DTC), 3

E, F

Exit strategy
- counterintuitive, 24
- long-term plans, 24
- pitch meeting, 25
- worst-case scenario, 25
- wrong signal, 25

G, H

General partners (GPs), 10

Go-to-market strategy

© Haje Jan Kamps 2020
H. J. Kamps, *Pitch Perfect*, https://doi.org/10.1007/978-1-4842-6065-4

Go-to-market strategy (*cont.*)
  marketing and segmentation, 63, 64
  "one-size-fits-all" solution, 61
  painting picture, solution, 62, 63

I, J

Investment
  company, good fit, 95
  thesis, 94
  wrong investor, 93
Investor, 1, 90
  firms, 85
  fund dynamics, 85
  information, 84
  notes field, 86
  partners, 84
  pretty broad approach, 87
  relevant, 85
  tier, 86

K

Key performance indicators (KPIs), 47

L

Lifetime value (LTV), 48, 57
Limited partners (LPs), 10, 94
LinkedIn, 90

M

Market
  venture-backable business, 39
  size, 42
    contextual approach, 39
    dynamics, 40
    market analysts, 40
    regional launch, 39
  trajectories
    digital photography, 41
    growing business, 41
    macroeconomic trends, 41
Minimum viable product (MVP)
  customer research, 51
  early-stage companies, 51
  product/market fit, 51
  quick product experiment, 50
  testing, 50

Moat, 24
  budget airlines, 55
  customers disagree, 55
  defense against competitors, 53
  innovations, 54
  music-streaming
      services, 54
  pain points, 54
  patents, 55
  trade secrets, 54
  weaker case, 54

N, O

Netflix, 58
Net promoter score (NPS), 50

P, Q, R

Patents, 54, 55
Pitch
  broad strokes, 32
  context, 31
  CRM, 29
  deck design
    begin/close, how to, 19, 20
    builds, 19
    critical design points, 18
    graphical design, 15
    high-altitude drone, 16
    high-end consumer, 17
    resources in-house, 18
    tools, 16
  emotional level, 28
  fundraising, 29
  groundbreaking/dramatic, 28
  investor, 31
  issues, 28
  lodging business, 32
  long-term vision, 33
  gig-economy transport, 31
Powerful moats
  market dynamics, 56
  network effect, 56
  platform effect, 56
Power purchase agreements, 59
Product/solution
  broader vision, 35
  customer feedback, 37

customer needs, 36
detail-oriented approach, 37
end-to-end solution, 36
longer-term goal, 36
macro/micro level, 37
milestones, 38
potential buyers, 38
scheduling, 36
use cases, 36

S

Serviceable available market (SAM), 42
Serviceable obtainable market (SOM), 42
Slides, pitches
beachhead market, 23
benefits, 26
broad strokes, 26
business model, 23
compelling narrative arc, 26
exit strategy, 24, 25
funds, 24
historical dots, 23
investor's attention, 26
Keynote/PowerPoint, 26
market landscape/competitors, 23
market size/trajectory, 22
moat, 24
operating plan, 24
pitching coach, 26
pricing model, 23
problem, 22
product/service, 22
solution, 22
team, 22
traction, 23
waymarkers, 21
Storytelling
audience, 5–7
BeerSub.com, 3
definition, 2
start, where to, 7, 8
weave, how to, 4, 5
words/pictures, 3
Superpower, 53

T

Team
founder-market fit, 43
initial assumptions, 44
most valuable asset, 43
risk reduction, 43
startups, 43
venture capital, 44
Timing
consumer-grade photography drones, 76
GPS and data network capabilities, 77
Internet-of-things company, 77
puck, 75
smartphones, 76
technological innovations, 77, 78
Total addressable market (TAM), 41
Traction, 23
CAC, 48
capitalization, 47
KPIs, 47
LTV, 48, 49
MVPs, 50
NPS, 50
primary metrics, 47
revenue, 47

U

Uber Eats, 31, 59

V

Venture capital (VC)
definition, 9
investment, 10, 11, 13
IPO, 12
LPs, 10
management fee/carried interest, 12, 13
principle, 10
raising money, 13
Venture-funding specific, 97

W, X, Y, Z

Wirecutter commissions, 58